Pojo's
Unofficial
TOTAL
Gundam Wing

TRIUMPH
ENTERTAINMENT
Division of Triumph Books
601 South LaSalle Street
Chicago, Illinois 60605

The Wide World of Gundam

At one time, we Gundam fans were viewed as a different breed of anime lovers. Sure, we wanted action just like everyone else, but we also wanted meaning with our action.

We wanted depth of character; we wanted unpredictable storylines; we wanted to be shocked and challenged. Most of all, we wanted more out of an animated television series.

Today, we aren't seen so much as a different breed but as a dominant one. Face it: Gundam fans are everywhere. Your next-door neighbor is a Gundam fan, your brother is a Gundam fan, you are a Gundam fan.

It's with you (and your next-door neighbor and your brother) in mind that we've published PoJo's World Gundam Special. This one-of-a-kind issue is devoted to every type of Gundam fan: old-school, new school, fans of Gundam Wing and fans of Z Gundam. We've also included special sections on video games, card games, model building, the characters, the mobile suits and more. There's even a comprehensive guide to every Gundam series, movie and original video animation, from 0079 to Turn-A. So, stand up and be counted, Gundam fans. You are the dominant breed!

PoJo

© 2000 Contents H&S Media, Inc. All Rights Reserved

Executive Editor . . . . Linc Wonham
Creative Director . . . . Ray Ramos
Editor-In-Chief . . . . PoJo (Bill Gill)
Managing Editor . . . . Nancy Davies
Managing Art Director . . . . Mark Styczen
Senior Editor . . . . Kit Kiefer
Senior Graphic Designer . . . . Robert A. Wyszkowski
Cover Design . . . . Kai's Kreations, Inc.

contents

4 Gundam Gossip
Cartoon Network must decide what to do with its juicy Toonami 'toons

8 Pilgrimage to Mecha
MechaPS is fighting to bring the Gundam dream to life

10 Gundam Timeline
A quick glance at all the Gundam series, movies and original video animations

14 The Gundam Legacy
An introduction to 20 years of Gundam sagas

49 The Third Dimension
View some of your favorite Gundam characters in 3-D splendor

66 Gundam Power
Gundam Wing is the strongest force in anime

72 The Politics of Gundam Wing
Gundam Wing's treatment of politics and ethics put it a cut above the rest

74 The Gundam Files
Vital stats and info on the key characters of Gundam Wing

84 Mobile Suit Mania
Get the goods on your favorite (or least favorite) mecha

96 G-Shock
A full-tilt Gundam Wing episode guide

102 Gundam War
A new Gundam TCG is finally out of the box

106 High Drama Gaming
Gundam Side Story 0079 will get your video-game motor runnin'

114 Invasion of the Plastic Warriors
In history and diversity, Gundam modeling is the only match for the anime sagas

Gundam Gossip

Cartoon Network isn't willing to set its Toonami 'toons free – just yet

By Kit Kiefer

When something is successful beyond its creators' wildest dreams, what do the creators do? In the non-TV world, they rejoice. In TV-land, they panic.

The subject of the latest panic is *Gundam Wing*. Cartoon Network has such a hot property on its hands that it's all aflutter trying to figure out where to go from here. Should the network bring over different storylines, move the time slot, go to theaters or start a whole new network built around *Gundam Wing* and its brethren – all anime, all the time?

Not a bad problem to have.

The network bosses do know the concept of more (as in, when a show is as popular as *Gundam Wing*, give the audience more to watch). And there's certainly no shortage of more to give them. *Gundam Wing* is just the nose of a sprawling Gundam giant that's been

The first episode of the *Gundam Wing W: Endless Waltz* cycle aired on Oct. 20.

nurtured in Japan for decades. Over there, Gundam story lines grow like zucchini plants, sending vines every which way. Some of the story lines are serious and straightforward, others are humorous, others are highly complicated. It's up to Cartoon Network to decide which ones will play over here.

Cartoon Network has made one big decision: On Oct. 20, the *Gundam Wing W: Endless Waltz* cycle aired. The three- episode special (officially titled *New Mobile Report Gundam W: Endless Waltz*) is a sort of sequel/prequel to the previously aired *Gundam Wing* episodes. It describes what happens to the pilots after the end of the main G-Wing story and incorporates flashbacks that outline the development of Operation Meteor, the plan that sent the Gundams to Earth. It also dishes some dirt on one of the Gundam pilots, but you'll have to watch to find out what and who.

The best news is that *Endless Waltz* should be an extremely hot addition to the already-smokin' Gundam series.

Cartoon Network must decide what to do with the successful *Gundam Wing* series.

There are 49 episodes of Gundam W translated into English, and all have aired on Cartoon Network. And you know what? They'll air again. Apparently, all you fans of ToonNet's wildly popular Toonami block don't mind reruns.

The real drama involves what other Gundam stuff will be added to the mix. Will it be the *Mobile Suit Gundam* or the *Mobile Suit Gundam G* – or neither? Cartoon Network wonders the same thing. And that's not the only thing it wonders about.

Bandai has announced the original *Mobile Suit Gundam* cartoons will air in North America in 2001. These 52

episodes are where it all began, Gundam-wise. They follow the exploits of the White Base Crew in the bitter war between the Earth Federation and the Duchy of Zeon. The characters may be new to most viewers and the animation may vary from the highly stylized anime of the current Gundam gems, but the plotlines will continue to involve young pilots battling overwhelming odds.

There's also a trilogy of movies that combines new footage and 42 episodes of the old cartoons. These are Japanese movies, so they're not as long or as polished as American theatrical releases. They could wind up in American

theaters, but they have more of the characteristics of made-for-TV movies.

All of the early Gundam material probably will wind up on Cartoon Network in some form. However, Bandai hasn't said for certain that the first Gundam storyline will air on Cartoon Network – it just said the episodes would air in North America in 2001 – and Cartoon Network hasn't said it would take the episodes if they were offered.

"Obviously, Gundam has been a very popular portion of our Toonami block, which has become very popular as a whole," said Laurie Goldberg, Cartoon ➜

Will *Mobile Suit Gundam G* be added to Cartoon Network's Toonami block?

If you're dying to catch up on viewing from Gundam's early days, be patient. All the material will probably run on Cartoon Network in some form.

Network's PR chief. "We're exceptionally pleased with Toonami. We're exceptionally pleased about Gundam as a part of Toonami. We have been in negotiation with Bandai for other Gundam story lines and are optimistic about our chances of airing new Gundam material. But that's really all we can say."

But Cartoon Network is saying a whole lot more about its original programming for the Toonami block, like the September-airing Intruder series, which lets viewers input help and determine the fate and deliverance of Tom, the host of Toonami.

Original programming is increasingly where it's at for Cartoon Network, as its original cartoons are attracting droves of viewers. That's one of the reasons Cartoon Network bumped most of its vast library of Hanna-Barbera cartoons to the new Boomerang network.

Cartoon Network's other big issue is also Boomerang related: Should Cartoon

Network spin off Toonami – the way it did the Hanna-Barbera library – into a network of its own? There's no all-anime network on the cable horizon, and Cartoon Network sure could give a Toonami Network a heavy-duty boost.

The Internet has been full of reports that a Toonami Network is coming soon. But Cartoon Network isn't so sure.

"I know there's been a lot of speculation about a Toonami network], but we don't have any immediate plans for anything like that," said Goldberg. "We just have to take one step at a time and focus on what we're doing with Toonami right now.

"We think the best way of showing our strong commitment to anime right now is through our Toonami block. I wouldn't rule out the possibility of our doing an anime network – you never know. But it's certainly not in our immediate future."

That's all right with fans, just so they keep some form of *Gundam Wing* coming. And as hot as it is, Cartoon Network would be crazy to stop now. ■

"We're exceptionally pleased with Toonami. We're exceptionally pleased about Gundam as part of Toonami."

– Laurie Goldberg, Cartoon Network PR chief

If a Toonami Network is born, Gundam will likely be its meal ticket.

Pilgrimage to Mecha

Somewhere south of Bakersfield, MechaPS is bringing the Gundam dream to life

By Kit Kiefer

Maybe the dialog in the frequently-asked-questions portion of the web site, www.MechaPS.com, said it best:

Q: Why?

Earle: Why not? To be cool. To be worshiped by nerds across the globe.

Lang: Gotta beat the military/NASA to the punch. Otherwise, we civilians will never get to use them. Besides this is Bakersfield. What else are we going to do other than build giant 'bots?

"Earle" is Earle Bishop, "Lang" is Lang Nelson, and they're in charge of engineering and aesthetics for one of the strangest do-it-yourself projects in recent memory: the effort to build an honest-to-goodness, real-life mech.

Now don't start thinking you ought to start saving so you can spring for one of these instead of a PlayStation 2. Bishop and Nelson and their merry band at MechaPS figure it'll be 25 years before a fully blown anime-style creation is mass-produced. On the other hand, prototypes exist. The actual metal-on-metal building should occur sometime this year and production models may roll out in 2002 if everything breaks right – which the developers think just might happen.

The mech currently on the drawing board is two-legged and stands about 25 feet tall. Its central structure of steel I-beams is covered with shells of circular metal and fiberglass or plastic. (Everything's pretty basic on the current drawing-board model; no swoopy fiberglass sheathing...yet.)

A conventional internal combustion engine will power the first mech, and core functions like walking and maintaining balance will be handled by a special blend of hardware and software.

Right now there are absolutely no plans to add big honking cannons to the mech. The developers will settle for having the

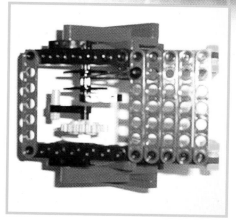

Tools of the mecha trade (clockwise from top): metal I-beams, standing mechanism, clutching system, engine

thing walk and turn and maintain its balance consistently. Bishop predicts that the mech's main use will be in construction and similarly dangerous civilian-sector jobs.

Nelson offers another viewpoint: "If this is successful, I would have a hard time not seeing the military interested in this project."

The other big thing on the MechaPS agenda is finding a place to build the thing. Right now, MechaPS is a glorified garage project. But with land secured south of Bakersfield for an engineering and production facility, and since third-party

funding is not a problem, MechaPS will be out of the garage soon.

Today the garage and tomorrow the world? Something like that. MechaPS' goals – a mecha in every home, or at least on every construction site, by 2025 – may seem fantastic, but the slow-and-steady way they're going about achieving those goals is anything but.

For the complete scoop on the mecha project, including an almost day-by-day log of the company's progress, check out www.MechaPS.com. ■

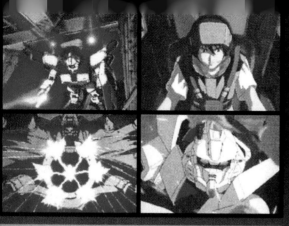

MOBILE SUIT GUNDAM
The 08th MS TEAM
October U.C. 0079 - December U.C. 0079

13 Episodes/30 minutes per episode

Federation Lieutenant Shiro Amada is transferred from the Space Unit to the Ground Unit, where he ends up leading the 08th MS team, a troubled group consisting of misfits and rogues. The Zeon Secret Weapon Development Unit has a base close to where the 08th MS Team is stationed. A female pilot, Aina Saharin, is the test pilot close to this threatening secret. She and Shiro have met before, when they were both adrift alone in space.

Released January 25, 1996

MOBILE SUIT GUNDAM 0800
War in the Pocket
December U.C. 0079 - January U.C. 0080

6 Episodes/30 minutes per episode

A young lieutenant of the Zeon's Special Unit, Bernie, secretly enters the neutral Space Colony Side 6, where he meets Al. He and the innocent boy become friends. Bernie also becomes attracted to Al's neighbor, the beautiful Chris. But Chris is in fact the female test pilot of the latest Gundam, which is exactly what Bernie's unit is trying to destroy.

Released March 25, 1989

MOBILE SUIT Z GUND
March U.C. 0087 - Februa
U.C. 0088

50 Episodes/30 minutes episode

This story chronicles the battle betwe the Titans, an elite troop of Federatic Forces who are obsessed with ruling and the AEUG, an organization dedic to preserving the rights of those livin Space (sometimes called Spacenoids) Camille Vidan, whose parents were k by the Titans, becomes the pilot of th

0079
MOBILE SUIT GUNDAM
The 08th MS Team

0080
MOBILE SUIT GUNDAM 0800
War in the Pocket

UNIVERSAL

0079
MOBILE SUIT GUNDAM

0083
MOBILE SUIT GUNDAM 0083
Stardust Memory

GUNDAM TIMELINE

MOBILE SUIT GUNDAM
June U.C. 0079 - December U.C. 0079

43 Episodes/30 minutes per episode

The Duchy of Zeon invents a gigantic human-shaped weapon called the Mobile Suit (MS) and begins its war for independence against the Federated Union of Earth. The story depicts the life of young boys and girls in the war, focusing on the young protagonist named Amuro Ray. Amuro becomes the pilot of the Gundam, a prototype MS developed by Federation Forces. Through his battles against the ace pilot of Zeon, Char Aznable, and the bitter trials of the war, he becomes aware of his uniqueness as a Newtype.

Aired April 7, 1979 - January 26, 1980

MOBILE SUIT GUNDAM 0083
Stardust Memory
October U.C. 0083 - December U.C. 0083

13 Episodes/30 minutes per episode

Three years after the end of the war between the Duchy of Zeon and the Federation Forces, a group called the Delaz Fleet is formed by the survivors of the Zeon army. Their goal is to rebuild Zeon. Its ace pilot, Major Anavel Gato, steals the Gundam GP02, a nuclear equipped model in development by the Federation. Lieutenant Kou Uraki pilots the Gundam GP01, the only one left, in an attempt to stop him. Operation Stardust, the plan of the Delaz Fleet, is such a large-scale operation that it shakes up the Federation

Released May 23, 1991

est MS, the Zeta Gundam, and rows himself into the war. A third oup known as Axis, consisting of the rvivors of the Duchy of Zeon, becomes volved in their battles.
ired March 2, 1985 -
ebruary 22, 1986

MOBILE SUIT GUNDAM
Char's Counterattack
December U.C. 0092 - March U.C. 0093
MOVIE
Char Aznable is now the general of Neo Zeon. He regards those who still live on Earth as the cause of all the battles and plots to drop the asteroid Axis on the Earth. In order to stop char, Amuro leads the troops of Lond Bell with his Gundam. The fate of the Earth and all its inhabitants is at stake, and the time has come to conclude the years of feuding between Amuro and Char.
Released March 12, 1988

MOBILE SUIT V GUNDAM
April U.C. 0153 - June U.C. 0153
52 Episodes/30 minutes per episode
Space Colony Side 2 calls itself the Zanscare Empire and begins conquering Earth territory. The League Militare resists the Space Colony onslaught and builds the V Gundam to help it fight. As pilot of V Gundam, 15-year-old Usso Evin becomes embroiled in the fight to save the world.
Aired April 2, 1993 - March 25, 1994

0087	0092	0153
MOBILE SUIT Z GUNDAM	**MOBILE SUIT GUNDAM**	**MOBILE SUIT V GUNDAM**
	Char's Counterattack	

1011110101010101010¦00010101010101010¦10010001010101¦100010101010100010¦10100¦10101010100

0088	0123
MOBILE SUIT ZZ GUNDAM	**MOBILE SUIT GUNDAM**
	F-91

CENTURY

MOBILE SUIT GUNDAM ZZ
March U.C. 0088 - January U.C. 0089
46 Episodes/30 minutes per episode
After winning the war, the Axis changes its name to Neo Zeon and plots to conquer the Earth. Judo Ashita, a young boy, joins the defeated AEUG and shows unprecedented talent as the pilot of the ZZ Gundam. The AEUG forms the Gundam Team to defend itself from Neo Zeon's attacks.
Aired March 7, 1986 - January 31, 1987

MOBILE SUIT GUNDAM F-91
March U.C. 0123
MOVIE
To build Cosmo Babylonia, a space nation ruled by aristocrats, Crossbone Vanguard — the private army of the Rohah's — attacks Space Colony Frontier Side. When his peaceful homeland is destroyed, high school student Seabook Arno pilots the latest Gundam model, the Gundam F-91, and joins the resistance.
Released March 16, 1991

MOBILE FIGHTER G GUNDAM

April Future Century 60 - March Future Century 61

49 Episodes/30 minutes per episode

G Gundam is set in an alternate universe using the Future Century timeline. The Gundam Fight is held among all the nations of the world every four years. Each nation sends its Gundam unit to the competition. For this tournament, a new rule has gone into effect: the champion will rule Earth for the next four years. But, behind the Thirteenth Gundam Fight, there is a huge conspiracy to destroy Earth.

Aired April 1, 1994 - March 31, 1995

ALTERNATE

GUNDAM SAGA

NEW MOBILE REPORT GUNDAM W: ENDLESS WALTZ

April, After Colony 197

3 Episodes/30 minutes per episode

The bitter battles are over, and the unified nation of Earth is born. The world is finally at peace … or so it seems. But, Marie Maia, the daughter of Treize, the former leader of OZ, declares war on the Earth. Heero, Duo and Quatre, who fought for peace once before, take up the challenge in their Gundams. But, in Marie Maia's army are their friends, Trowa and Wufei.

Released January 25, 1997

EW MOBILE REPORT
UNDAM W

il After Colony 195 - March A.C. 196

Episodes/30 minutes per episode

is another alternate universe story. The
et Society OZ oppresses space immigrants
er the guise of unifying the Earth's territory.
of the Colonies, L1 through L5, send their
dams to Earth to attack OZ. Guerilla war
ts between the two factions. In this war
een Space and Earth,

TURN-A GUNDAM

51 Episodes/30 minutes per episode

Turn-A Gundam marks the first Gundam project involving creator
Yoshiyuki Tomino since *Gundam F91*. This story centers around
Rolan, a boy who descends to Earth from space. He attempts to fit in
with the people around him and eventually gets a job as a driver for
a wealthy family. But Rolan is also the pilot of the Turn-A Gundam.
What are they doing on Earth? Stay tuned, and find out.
Currently Airing in Japan

10111101010101010101001010101010101010010010010010010010010010100010101001001010100

UNIVERSE

AFTER WAR GUNDAM X

After War 0015 - 0016

39 Episodes/30 minutes per episode

The Seventh Space War involved the entire Earth territory, and the
damage was devastating. Fifteen years after the end of this war,
young Garrod Ran, who lives in the wasteland, meets Tiffa, a
Newtype girl who is being chased by the Space Revolution Army. To
protect Tiffa, Garrod gets ahold of Gundam X, one of the most powerful weapons used in the war.

Aired April 5, 1996 - December 28, 1996

The Gundam Legacy

An introduction to 20 years of Gundam sagas

By Colin Liu

Gundam fever is a relatively new thing for North American anime fans. But across the big Western pond, Asian sci-fi and anime fans know all about Gundam, and have for most of the last two decades. Two decades of Gundam? Oh, yes – and here's the proof: reviews of every Gundam series aired in Japan and abroad, from the *Mobile Suit Gundam 0079* to *Turn-A Gundam*. We think this will help you appreciate the depth of Japan's greatest sci-fi anime saga. Enjoy!

The Gundam Legacy

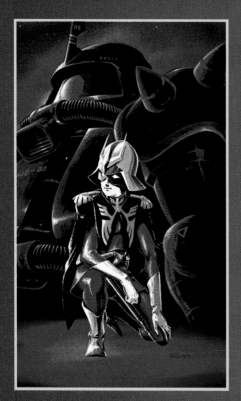

0079 Gundam pilot Amuro Ray, with the head of RX-78-2 Gundam in the background.

0079 ace pilot Char Aznable.

Mobile Suit Gundam

(0079) – TV series and movie trilogy

The original Gundam anime series made its Japanese debut in 1979. It was the brainchild of Kiyuki Tomino (now known as Yoshiyuki Tomino), who had been the animator of Hayao Miyazaki's famous *Heidi* TV series.

The story was set in a post-A.D. 2045 era known as the Universal Century (UC), a time when humans had successfully transferred their excess population into space colonies – giant cylindrical satellites divided into different groups (or "Sides").

As time passed, the space colonists began to assert their independence from the corrupt and indifferent Earth Federation, which maintained sovereignty over the space colonies. The simmering crisis erupted in January UC 0079, when the Principality of Zeon, an authoritarian and ultra-nationalist state based in Side 3, declared itself independent and waged a devastating war (later known as the One-Year War) against the Earth Federation.

The *Mobile Suit Gundam* episodes take place at the height of the conflict in September UC 0079, when the Zeons, equipped with mobile suits (giant humanoid combat robots), attack the previously peaceful Side-7 colony just as the Federal Force was testing its latest weapons to counter the Zeon's advances.

Amuro Ray, an introverted 15-year-old civilian and son of a Federal Force engineer, witnesses Zeon's vicious attack on his home colony and fights back by piloting a Gundam, the Federal Force's secret weapon which was being tested in Side-7. His attack gets the story rolling, as it attracts a diverse group of young civilians and reserve soldiers who eventually became the Federation's ace combat unit – and the heroes of the *0079* saga.

Its militaristic undertone is what makes *0079* unique. No nice-guy robots with lonesome heroes bucking the odds against enormous armies of fiendish-looking bad guys here. Instead, Gundam is only a small part of a gigantic military organization fighting a real and menacing military threat (Zeon).

Viewers of all ages have no problem comparing the One Year War to World War II and other global military conflicts, making *0079* a breath of fresh (if not altogether happy) air and a welcome break from the often predictable '70s super-robot animes. Amuro and his friends are heroes, but they can't win the war by themselves. Tomino emphasized that wars are won over time, not overnight. That's still a rare concept in sci-fi and anime. ➜

The Gundam Legacy

Gundam creator Yoshiyuki Tomino crafted characters who had much more depth than those found in a standard anime series.

0079 characters (left to right) Matilda Ajane, Marai Yashima and Amuro Ray, with Gundam in shooting pose in the background.

Then there are the mobile suits. Thanks to the skillful design of mecha ace Kunio Okawara, these gigantic robots are no longer the one-off bad guys of '70s anime series like *Mazinger Z* or the original *Getter Robo* series. Instead, both the Fed's and Zeon's MS are mass-produced machines dispatched in squadrons to counter the enemies – and their designs still captivate viewers. What's more, *0079* is perhaps the first TV series in anime history where the names of the mechas aren't shown on the TV screen or shouted out by someone during attacks. It may not be such a big deal now, but back then it won over the hearts and minds of many dissatisfied sci-fi viewers all across Asia.

Another endearing element about *0079* is its realism. Almost all the characters are as realistic as you and I, so viewers are drawn into the Gundam World as witnesses, watching history unfold before their eyes. You can sense the coldness deep inside young Amuro's heart under his hot-blooded, anti-war fatigue; you dislike "Red Comet" Char Aznable, the villain, yet you understand his desire for revenge against Zeon's royal

family and his affection for Sayla Mass, his estranged sister.

Tomino emphasizes light-at-the-end-of-the-tunnel themes, yet allows us a lot of freedom to ponder the possibilities: What would happen next? Is there really a clear-cut good guy and bad guy? Do the spacenoids (Newtypes) represent hope for the future?

Such freedom and ambiguity seldom appears in the sci-fi world, yet they've become the trademarks of Tomino's subsequent Gundam series.

An epic and groundbreaking TV show, *Gundam 0079* is a highly recommended must-watch. While the original 43-episode TV series was not very well-received in Japan initially, subsequent reruns drew an ever-growing army of viewers and became so popular that the TV series was retooled into a three-part motion picture released in 1981.

The movie trilogy – *Mobile Suit Gundam* (1981), *Soldiers of Sorrow* (1981) and *Encounters in Space* (1982) – is made up mostly of footage from the TV series, plus new animation directed by Yoshikazu Yasuhiko. It's a decent add-and-subtract

exercise which faithfully follows the One Year War storyline. The core characters and mechas are retained, and more detailed re-animations, re-recorded soundtracks and new theme songs are added. While it's hard for a six-hour movie trilogy to preserve the original spirit of the classic TV series, it's still a good introduction to the world of UC Gundam.

Mobile Suit Z Gundam – TV series

For writer/director Yoshiyuki Tomino and production company Nippon Sunrise, the popularity of the *Gundam 0079* TV series in the early 1980s was totally unexpected. To cater to fans' demands, Tomino rushed out a retooled six-hour movie trilogy and followed it up in 1985 with the *Z Gundam* TV series. ➔

The Gundam Legacy

Z Gundam is regarded as the second most important Gundam series right after *0079*. The 50-episode saga fast-forwards to UC 0087, seven years after the conclusion of the cataclysmic One Year War. Peace exists on the surface, but the hostility between the independence-minded space colonists and the corrupt and incompetent Federation government is thicker than ever. The Titans – an elite force created by the Federation in UC 0083 to hunt down renegade Zeons and brutally suppress anti-Federation movements in the colonies – are everywhere, harassing the colonists while secretly building up their strength for the eventual domination of space colonies and the Federation.

Mankind's only hope rests with a resistance movement called the Anti-Earth Union Group, an umbrella group consisting of former Zeon soldiers, disgruntled Federal Forces and colonial sympathizers. Backed by powerful conglomerates, AEUG quietly gathers its strength before taking on the Titans.

AEUG forces the action when Quattro Vezina (the captain of AEUG's mobile-suit force, but in reality the former Zeon ace pilot Char Aznable) leads a carefully planned operation to capture the Titans' newly developed Gundams, which were being tested in the Side-7 "Green Noah" colony. Things go haywire when Camille Vidan – a naive 17-year-old high-school student thrown in jail by the Titans for petty offenses – hops onto one of the Titans' Gundam and seeks asylum with Quattro's forces.

Tragedy then strikes when Camille's parents are killed by Titans, and the grief-stricken young man joins AEUG. In the ensuing 11 months of battle known as the Gryps War, Camille's life is changed forever. He crosses paths with former Gundam ace Amuro Ray, scheming Zeon royalist Haman Khan and ambitious Titans officer Paptimus Scirocco. He also has an ill-fated love affair with the artificially enhanced Newtype, Four Murasame.

Tragic events and hard-fought battles hone Camille's Newtype ability to an unprecedented level, but it also begins to affect his mental well-being as the final battles loom between AEUG, the Titans, Haman and Scirocco. Can Camille, Quattro and AEUG end this human tragedy and bring peace to humankind?

With all these great ingredients in place, Tomino was able to create an epic sci-fi saga that's every bit as rich as its predecessor. Tomino further questions what the future holds for our living planet, and this time his answers are much more ominous, yet still ambiguous.

Not merely a glorious sequel to the classic *0079*, *Z Gundam* is also the turning point for future UC Gundam series. It's a definite must-watch. ➜

Camille Vidan – a naive 17-year-old high-school student, hops onto one of the Titans' Gundam and seeks asylum with Quattro's forces.

Unlike its ominous predecessor, *ZZ* features the typical wide-eyed anime style.

Mobile Suit Gundam ZZ – TV series

Following the dark and gloomy *Z Gundam* series, writer/director Yoshiyuki Tomino lightened things up a bit with *Gundam ZZ*. Since its release in 1986, *ZZ* remains one of the most controversial Gundam series. But it's also an essential part of Tomino's UC Gundam saga.

ZZ's story picks up where *Z* left off. After the intense and grueling Gryps War, Haman Khan and her Zeon royalists emerge victorious – and with the Titans finally out of the picture, the ambitious young woman can put into motion her plans for space domination. Operating from the giant asteroid fortress Axis and appointing herself the regent to the lone surviving young heir of Zeon's royal family, Haman revives the Principality of Zeon, now known as Neo Zeon, and launches a multi-pronged operation to gain the support of space colonies against the Earth Federation.

Haman still considers AEUG – its strength seriously weakened by the Gryps War – a major threat to her master plan, so she orders her troops to root out the remaining AEUG forces, starting with its flagship, Ahgama. The Neo Zeons intercept Ahgama inside Side-1's "Shangri-La" colony, but by chance Ahgama is saved by a 14-year-old named Judeau Ashta.

To give his young sister Lina a better life and an education, Judeau and his friends leave their poverty-stricken home colony and join Ahgama. Judeau dislikes war and all things military, but he springs into action when Lina is captured by the Neo Zeons, determined to rescue his sister and bring peace to mankind.

To balance out *Z Gundam*'s gloom and doom, Tomino opted to pack *ZZ* with typical wide-eyed anime-style humor. But the militant audio-video elements are still there, with character design by Yukihiro Kitazume, mecha designs by Makoto Kobayashi and Yutaka Izubuchi and music by Shigeaki Saegusa.

All told, *Gundam ZZ* plays an important role in UC Gundam history. If you want to understand the whole of the Gundam world, it's something you ought to check out.

Char's Counterattack – motion picture

After *Gundam ZZ*, writer/director Yoshiyuki Tomino closed out the post-One Year War UC trilogy in March 1988 with *Char's Counterattack*. This thrilling two-hour movie settles the long-standing feud between the famous antagonists from *0079*: Amuro Ray and "Red Comet" Char Aznable. Quattro Vezina (Char Aznable) mysteriously disappears at the end of *Z Gundam* but resurfaces as the leader of the second Neo Zeon and is determined to fulfill his father's prophecy of Newtype evolution at all costs. ➔

The eye-pleasing character designs alone make *0080* worth watching.

Realizing the imminent threat of Char's plan, Amuro, now a member of the Federal Force's elite task force Londo Bell, goes against Char with everything he has. The result is a personal showdown with the fate of the Earth at stake.

The final part of Tomino's One Year War trilogy bypasses the gloom of *Z Gundam* and the unusual nature of *Gundam ZZ* and goes straight for the adrenaline – and hits it dead-center.

CCA features a fast-paced but easily understandable story that even the *0079* fans who've missed both the *Z* and *ZZ* series will have no problem following. Under Yukihiro Kitazume's character design, both Amuro and Char mature with grace; their words and actions are those of

adults. No less impressive are the machines of mecha designer Yutaka Izubuchi and the music of composer Shigeaki Saegusa.

This near-perfect conclusion to the UC saga freed Tomino to create a new UC era to challenge the hearts and minds of Gundam fans. For that alone, the glorious Char's Counterattack deserves a special place in Gundam animation history.

Mobile Suit Gundam 0080: War in the Pocket – original video animation

From its inception until 1988, the Gundam universe was solely the creation of Yoshiyuki Tomino. Starting with *Gundam 0080*, Tomino opened his

universe to others – with stunning results.

Released in early 1989 to commemorate Gundam's 10th anniversary, *Gundam 0080* was the first Gundam series that was neither written nor directed by Tomino. The directing torch was passed on to Fumihiko Takayama, a veteran writer/director best-known for his work in *Macross Plus, Orguss 02* and *Bubblegum Crisis*.

Unlike the previous epics, *0080* was a six-episode mini-series released as original video animation in various formats. Instead of moving the UC timeline forward, *0080* was the first Gundam series to look back at the cataclysmic One Year War and tell a "side story" – a previously untold portion of the Gundam saga.

The story begins with a failed attempt by Zeon's elite Cyclops Team task force to capture the Federal Force's newest Gundam at the North Pole. The chase continues from Earth into space, where the focus falls onto Alfred Izuruha, a 10-year-old boy from the Side-6 space colony of Libot.

The *0080* series is an eyewitness account of this brutal war from Alfred's perspective. Gundam and other war machines are relegated to a minor role, and a female military officer (Chris MacKenzie) and a green Zeon rookie (Bernie Wiseman) provide the battle tension.

Visually, the beautiful character designs of Haruhiko Mikimoto (known for his famous work in Macross/Robotech) and mecha designs of Yutaka Izubuchi, Yasushi Ishizu, Mika Akitaka and →

The Gundam Legacy

The success of *0080* created a brand-new direction for Gundam sagas, but *0083* proved to be a confusing and unpopular follow-up effort.

Kasuhisa Kondo are worth watching all by themselves. Add Tetsuro Kashibuchi's unique and strong soundtrack and touching theme songs by vocalist Megumi Shiina, and you have a Gundam show certainly unlike the ones we used to know.

Much of the focus of *0080* is on characters, and not just Alfred. Here, almost every character is truly lifelike, and the smart and clear-cut execution of the story makes *0080* the kind of gripping prime-time drama that even non-Gundam fans will marvel at.

The friendship between Al, Chris and Bernie, under Takayama's skillful direction, is the story's most intriguing and touching aspect. Second-line characters are just as impressive, from Zeon's Steiner Hardy and his all-pro Cyclops Team, to his buddy/Zeon spy Charlie the barkeeper and the paraplegic Dr. Dick Ramo.

Thankfully, the darkness of the One Year War is balanced by the young and tender heart of Alfred who, through his traumatic experience, learns a valuable life lesson. The message that children are the pillar of a better future is a powerful and positive booster shot for every viewer's mind.

Despite the lesser role of Gundam and mechas, *0080* boasts some of the most impressive and memorable MS combat scenes; they're crisp, realistic and to the point. The strong re-establishment of the Zeons as fascist aggressors also clicks with viewers. Kashibuchi's music topped with Shiina's refreshing title songs help create just the right atmosphere.

For a six-episode-only mini-series, *Gundam 0080* is everything you'd want: neat, precise and affectionate. A classic.

Mobile Suit Gundam 0083: Stardust Memory – original video animation

For a long time, the term "Gundam" meant year-long, high-quality TV series created by Yoshiyuki Tomino. The unexpected success of *Gundam 0080* opened up a brand-new direction for Gundam sagas, yet it also showed that Gundam fans like sagas best. So the next logical step for Nippon Sunrise was to create another epic OVA (original video animation), which it did.

Gundam 0083: Stardust Memory was released in 1990, one year after the release of *Gundam 0080*. It's the second Gundam OVA that was neither written nor directed by Tomino.

Both *0080* and *0083* are side stories related to the One Year War, but the similarities end there. First of all, *0083* is a longer series (13 episodes compared to a mere six for *0080*, with more room and time to present its story and link the original *Gundam* (UC 0079) to *Z Gundam* (UC 0087).

Under the directorship of Takashi Imanishi, *0083* is the non-stop, action-packed story of a small group of diehard Zeon forces led by the shrewd and patient Aiguille Delaz. Its central theme is how the revenge on the victorious Earth Federation was concluded.

Compared to the heavy humanism of *0080*, *0083* is pure high-octane, Hollywood-style MS combat action straight out of Top Gun. Toshihiro Kawamoto, the show's character designer, →

The Gundam Legacy

At first, the characters also may be tough for long-time fans to embrace. The *0083* series is full of distant characters, while other Gundam series thrived on lively, flesh-and-blood characters.

No matter how good Kawamori and Katoki's mecha designs are, no matter how exciting the action sequences are, and no matter how sweet the theme songs are to the audience, they come too late to save *0083* from being one of the bleakest moments in Gundam animation history.

Gundam 0083 has all the ingredients to make it everlasting and memorable. Instead, what was intended to be as epic as *0079* and *Z Gundam* will forever be known as the Gundam series that failed to deliver.

Things didn't get much better with *Last Blitz of Zeon*, a two-hour movie version of the *Stardust Memory* OVA. Released in summer 1992, Last Blitz preserved *0083*'s faults and spoiled fans with a preview of the series conclusion. If you don't count the two new theme songs and a couple of new animation sequences at the opening, that's about it.

Last Blitz was the last chance for *0083*'s creative crew to improve on the series. But few improvements were made, and Gundam fans were left with a rare disappointment.

Mobile Suit Gundam F91 –motion picture

When Char's Counterattack neatly closed out the OYW saga, it allowed Gundam creator Yoshiyuki Tomino to unleash a brand-new chapter in UC history with *Gundam F91*. Released exactly three years after the debut of CCA, *Gundam F91* is another two-hour theatrical release aimed to give long-time UC Gundam fans a surprise, albeit with mixed results.

The time is now UC 0123, 30 years after the second Neo Zeon's armed struggle against the Earth Federation. →

presents a cast of diverse characters who are instantly familiar with long-time Gundam fans. They're complemented by sparkling mecha designs by veteran designer Shoji Kawamori and bright new star Hajime Katoki (who later designed the mechs for *V Gundam, Gundam Wing: Endless Waltz* and *The 08th MS Team*). The show features gripping soundtracks by Mitsuo Hagita, plus six theme songs featuring a variety of popular J-Pop and R&B artists. In short, Sunrise hoped *0083* would bring the Gundam saga to more casual audiences while still pleasing the hard-core fans.

The formula worked perfectly as *0083* remains one of the best-selling Gundam OVAs and has pleased fans worldwide, particularly those new to Gundam. The non-stop, one-on-one mecha combats include one Gundam versus another

Gundam for the first time, plus a massive nuclear attack and a spectacular battle between two mammoth mobile armors. What's more, fans were rocked by the hard-hitting opening theme songs one instant and soothed by the smoochy R&B ending themes the next.

At the other end of the spectrum, however, many long-time Gundam fans who grew up with Tomino's Gundam saga began to grumble at *0083*. They weren't upset by the obvious qualities noted above, but by the confusing storyline. Some important events are never clearly explained or answered. What's the true motive behind Cima Garahau's defection to the Federal Force? Who's the real puppetmaster(s) behind Operation Stardust? And how can the mobile-suit technology of *0083* fit into the *Z Gundam* era?

The Gundam Legacy

People on Earth and in space have healed many of the physical and mental wounds left by the previous century's endless wars; the construction of new space colonies is finally completed and the colonies are realigned into different "Sides" and "Frontiers." However, peacetime provides another golden opportunity for space-dwelling revolutionaries to rise again in their struggle for independence from the oppressive Earth Federation.

Nothing could prepare Seabrook Arno – a 17-year-old engineering student and a native of Frontier 4 space colony – and his friends for the occupation of their home colony by the Crossbone Vanguard (CV for short), an elite mobile-suit force and private army trained and financed in secret by the aristocratic Ronah family. The Ronahs are dedicated to establish an ideal society called "Cosmo Babylonia," in which mankind is led by only the best, the wisest and most courageous nobles instead of the corrupt politicians of the Earth Federation.

The teenagers escaped with the retreating Federal forces to the nearby Frontier 1 industrial colony, with the CV in hot pursuit. In desperation, the ragtag force chooses Seabrook to pilot *Gundam F91* – an advanced prototype mobile suit – in a counterattack. His unexpected success leads the Fed to explore his latent Newtype ability. Further battles ensue, and in the process Seabrook is reunited with his girlfriend Cecily Fairchild, who was lost in the CV's attack on Frontier 4 but is later revealed to be the heir of the Ronah family.

Together they discover the hidden agenda of Karozo "The Iron Mask" Ronah, Cecily's father and CV's commander-in-chief. Karozo has secretly developed a lethal weapon to eliminate the surplus population in space and eventually on Earth. It's up to the young lovers and *Gundam F91* to keep the madman's dream from coming true.

While *F91* seems to suggest a new direction for future Gundam sagas, it's actually very similar to the classic *Gundam 0079*. Although *F91* does include a new timeline, a new character and new mecha designs, and it's topped with high-quality animation.

F91 also represents a reunion of sorts: Tomino gets back together with character designer Yoshikazu Yasuhiko and mecha designer Kunio Okawara. Together, they create something new, yet familiar, to long-time Gundam fans. Okawara's radical MS design irks some fans who long for the mono-eyed bad guy MS, and the movie's short length and swift conclusion left some fans yearning for more of the quality flick.

But this desire gets satisfied with the release of *Crossbone Gundam*, a thrilling six-volume manga series written and illustrated by Hiroichi Hasegawa. *Crossbone Gundam* fills in the spaces between *F91* and the soon-to-follow *V Gundam* TV series.

If you want to experience what the new UC Gundam saga is all about, then *F91* is highly recommended.

Mobile Suit V Gundam – TV Series

The tradition of Tomino-written Gundam TV series returned in 1993 with *V Gundam*, a year-long epic UC Gundam saga set in UC 0153, 30 years after the revolt of *Gundam F91's* Crossbone Vanguard.

The corrupt and incompetent Earth Federation is once again facing a new ➜

Although *F91* seems to take a new direction, it borrows many themes from the original Gundam series.

The Gundam Legacy

Some of the characters in *V Gundam* resemble those from other series, such as *Gundam ZZ* (pictured below).

cherished and nurtured. The evolution of Newtypes – another constant of Tomino's Gundam world – also hinges on the young ones (Usso and his soul mate Shakti Karin) who have the greatest chance of helping humanity. Usso's awakening as a Newtype brings back fond memories of Amuro Ray in *0079*, and Shakti's effort to bring peace to mankind will make you marvel at Tomino's cleverness.

The importance of women is another dominant theme in this show; from the headstrong Mavette Fingerhut and the saintly Queen Maria to the cynical-turned-fanatical Katerjina Loos, Tomino's women are impact-makers. Moreover, your eyes will sparkle as you recognize some unique characters with familiar traits from other Gundam series: Just when you think Griffon is another Cima Garahau, she turns into a familiar *Gundam ZZ*-esque character.

The mecha design in *V Gundam* is perhaps the most controversial of all the Gundam series' designs. It features some of the most hideous mechas in the UC Gundam universe, ranging from ➡

military threat from a group of space colonists called the Zanscare Empire, which brutally suppresses those who oppose it. This eventually leads to a full-scale invasion of Earth with the aim of achieving what the Zeons failed to accomplish 74 years ago.

With the Feds once again hapless in the face of the Zanscare's advances, the daunting task of saving Earth falls to the League Militaire, a civilian-led resistance force. *V Gundam* is the story of how Usso Evin, a 13-year-old teenager awaiting his parents' return from space, unknowingly is drawn into this vicious military conflict and eventually becomes League Militaire's best hope against the Zanscares.

Running at a record-breaking 51 episodes, *V Gundam* resembles the previous UC Gundam sagas. Tomino reminds viewers this is still his world, yet he lets other writers' Gundam elements be included in his show.

With bigger budgets (including some of the best orchestral music in Gundam animation, courtesy of composer Akira Senju) and a full-year airing period,

Tomino added an extra touch of folklore and mysticism, and some real surprise, to the real-life elements of the UC Gundam saga. The story of a teenager who reluctantly becomes a mobile suit pilot and the fight for peace and justice are no strangers to Gundam fans, but Usso Evin's adventure is presented in a clever and convincing style, so edgy viewers will settle down quickly.

The David vs. Goliath style conflict will quickly remind viewers of the grueling Gryps War in *Z Gundam*, only this time the David (the lean but feisty League Militaire) is up against a Goliath (the Zanscare Empire) much more menacing than the Zeons or the Titans.

Through the eyes of Usso and his peers, Tomino amplifies his message of childhood innocence and the brutality of war. No character in the show is spared from the matter of life and death, and death is constantly knocking and comes quickly.

Still, the children's hearts and minds remain pure from start to end, and it's Tomino's intention to present the young generation as the hope of the future to be

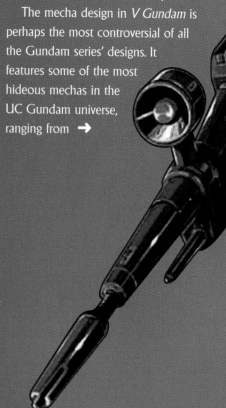

Gundam Wing

The Gundam Legacy

The *Mobile Fighter G-Gundam* series was released in time for Gundam's 15th anniversary celebration in 1994.

G-Gundam, the first non-UC series, was written and directed by famed robo-show veteran Yasuhiro Imagawa.

G-Gundam was a stark contrast to the other Gundam animations in almost every way, from its story to its music.

the unfathomable (Sandhog, a spider-like mobile worker) to the impossible (Doggorla, Zanscare's dragon-shaped mobile armor).

But don't forget that V's mecha designs were the collective works of Kunio Okawara (*0079*), Hajime Katoki (*0083*) and Junya Ishigaki. Together they created a new generation of Gundams on one hand and a new series of enemy MS with distinct design features on the other. Take a closer look and you'll see there are some ties to the One Year War, too: *V Gundam's* Core Fighter has a strong *0079* flavor, and Zanscare's MS Zoloatt and Zollidia are reprises of Zeon's MS Zaku II from the classic One Year War era.

The show's fast-paced and ferocious mecha combats also justify the existence of such imaginative designs as a transformable MS/helicopter gunship with beam rotors or an amphibious battleship with steamroller-like wheels. They aren't as childish as you may expect; after all, space colonies and all things futuristic are Tomino's pet loves, and in *V Gundam* they are beautifully presented. The Angel Halo – Zanscare's ultimate weapon of mass destruction – is unforgettable.

With *V Gundam*, Tomino proves his creativity is stronger than ever. It's not for the faint-hearted, but if you appreciate the man's genius, *V Gundam* certainly fulfills every Gundam fan's expectations. This is a real gem.

Mobile Fighter G-Gundam – TV series

After the conclusion of Tomino's intense and grueling *V Gundam* TV series, loyal Gundam fans – who felt a little emotionally drained after the UC saga – were suddenly snapped awake by its follow-up, *Mobile Fighter G-Gundam*.

Released in time for Gundam's 15th birthday celebration in 1994, *G-Gundam* was a significant departure from the previous Gundam animations in almost every way: story, timeline, technology,

writer, music and animation style.

G-Gundam's roots are in the hot-blooded, action-packed super-robot series so popular in mid-'70s Japan. But it's been warmly accepted by Gundam fans as one of the Gundam series that best preserves Tomino's philosophy and humanistic ideals.

Billed as the first-ever non-UC Gundam animation series, *G-Gundam* was written and directed by Yasuhiro Imagawa, a famous robo-show veteran best known for his "Giant Robo" animations. His bold experiment, fusing the militaristic Gundam story with a surreal mix of super-robot elements and contemporary martial-arts anime, resulted in a cartoon-style animated series with an engrossing story.

The time is now FC60, and numerous space colonies have been built to handle Earth's skyrocketing population. Endless quarrels and distrust between nations leads to a desire for universal domination, and the only thing that holds this desire in check is a special martial-arts tournament called "Gundam Fight" held every four years. For Gundam Fight, each space nation selects its best fighter to pilot its own gigantic combat robot and compete in a no-holds-barred, free-for-all contest with only one winner. FC60 marks the 13th Gundam Fight.

Domon Kasshu, Neo-Japan's Gundam Fighter and one of the strongest contenders to win the Fight, has other things on his mind. His father, a renowned scientist who creates the DG cells (a breakthrough in biotechnology which allows self-rehabilitation, self-improvement and self-evolution), disappears at the onset of the tournament, along with Devil Gundam, the monstrous, indestructible creature built with DG cells.

The future of mankind rests on Domon and the like-minded Gundam Fighters, all of whom are racing against time and each other before the Devil Gundam destroys the universe. ➔

The Gundam Legacy

While the Gundam in *0079* is only a small part of the military scheme, the Gundams in GW are the ultimate weapons.

G-Gundam is more than just a dime-a-dozen super-robot series. It features superb character design by Hiroshi Osaka and unforgettable mecha design by the incomparable trio of Kunio Okawara, Hajime Katoki and newcomer Kimitoshi Yamane. Topped off by highly charged and brooding orchestral soundtracks by the talented composer Kohei Tanaka, *G-Gundam* has all the right ingredients to be something special.

The master stroke, however, lies with Imagawa's creativity and through understanding of Tomino's philosophy, reflected in the portrayal of Domon's martial-arts teacher/arch-rival Master Asia. Master Asia may seem like a typical archvillain at first, but as the show develops, his love for and dedication to preserving the Earth makes him perhaps the show's most outstanding character.

G-Gundam is a unique blend of super-robot action and timeless philosophy. It stands apart from the other Gundam sagas and commands an altogether different level of respect. An excellent show!

New Mobile Report Gundam Wing – TV series

After *G-Gundam's* brilliant expansion of the Gundam universe, Nippon Sunrise, the company that owns and co-creates all Gundam animations, was convinced the name "Gundam" equalled "can't-miss" to anime fans, so it ventured even further away from the core Gundam sagas. This time the result was 1995's *Gundam Wing* – the worldwide smash Nippon Sunrise had been hoping for.

The second non-UC Gundam series, *Gundam Wing* boosted Gundam's popularity to an all-time high in Japan and has won millions of converts around the world.

Gundam Wing is unquestionably the most popular Gundam storyline ever created, but is it the best? Maybe. Maybe not.

Gundam Wing is, at its core, just one more part of the long-standing Gundam saga created by Yoshiyuki Tomino back in 1979. His vision and philosophy on "Gundam" allows other writers and directors to create their own version of Gundam – as long as it fits nicely into

Tomino's Gundam universe without any hint of contradiction.

To understand how *Gundam Wing* conforms, all you have to do is look at *Gundam Wing's* storyline, setting, characters and plot twists.

Gundam Wing's storyline closely parallels the original *Gundam 0079* series, with its epic military conflicts between the freedom-seeking space colonists and the oppressive/indifferent Earth dominators. Both series feature extremely similar characters (Char Aznable and Zechs Merquise, for example) and military hardware (Gundams). Last but not least, both series feature secret power struggles between the warring factions.

But before you start thinking *Gundam Wing* is just an imitation of the original classic, stop right there. Under the skillful writing and directing of Masashi Ikeda (of *Ronin Warriors* and *Darkstalkers* fame), *Gundam Wing* successfully combines the grueling UC military conflicts with some delicate subtleties. ➜

The 1995 *Gundam Wing* made the saga an international hit.

The Gundam Legacy

Gundam X aims to combine the best of *Gundam Wing* and the UC Gundam sagas.

While the Gundam in *0079* is only a small part of a gigantic military establishment where the outcome of war is determined by tactics and time, the Gundams in GW are ultimate weapons. Their five young pilots have the weight of the world on their shoulders and have been trained to bring peace to the universe all by themselves. This super-robot-esque approach has echoes of *G-Gundam*, yet it works to near-perfection in the GW's After Colony era.

Another feature unique to *Gundam Wing* is Relena Peacecraft, the peace-loving/seeking character whose persistence in bringing peace through non-violent means is unprecedented in Gundam animation history. In *Gundam 0079* and other UC series, the only way to make peace was through war.

Gundam Wing inherits the spirit of the UC Gundam sagas but adds a unique spin that makes it a refreshing and excellent series all by itself. If you've just become a Wing fan, you'll be surprised and mesmerized by the equally fantastic world of the UC Gundam sagas. If you're a diehard UC fan who still holds a grudge against alternate-universe Gundam series,

give *Gundam Wing* a try; you'll be surprised. *Gundam Wing* works both ways.

After War Gundam X – TV series

Closely following the mega-success of *Gundam Wing*, *After War Gundam X* was the third and supposedly final non-UC Gundam animation series. Like its predecessors, *Gundam X* was an ambitious attempt to present Gundam in a unique style. Though the result is a far cry from *G-Gundam* or *Gundam Wing*, it remains an important component in the history of Gundam animation as well as the final piece of the puzzle for Yoshiyuki Tomino, helping to unify all the different Gundam universes with his latest *Turn-A Gundam* animation series.

Aired in 1996, this 39-episode TV series is set in a postwar world vastly different from that of the UC, FC and AC eras. The time is now After War (AW) 15, 15 years after the catastrophic 7th Space War, where the separatist Space Revolutionary Army waged a devastating war against the dominating (Old) Earth Federation. The war ended in chaos and carnage and reduced the Earth to an

anarchic wasteland run by warlords, feudal rulers and scavenger groups like the Vultures, who survive by picking at the carcasses of the fallen.

Jamil Neate, captain of the Vultures' flagship Freedom and a veteran of the last war, uses his current job to search for and protect Newtypes, human beings with paranormal abilities who are hotly pursued by both former warring factions in preparation for a new conflict. One such Newtype is Tiffa Adill, a young girl who was chased by the agents of the New Federation government but was rescued by Garrod Ran, a 15-year-old street urchin who lost his parents in the last war and makes his living scavenging scrap military hardware.

By sheer luck, Garrod discovers *Gundam X*, a highly advanced mobile suit made by the Old Federal Force in the last war. Together with Tiffa, Garrod gambles and pilots the Gundam and successfully repels the attacking New Federal Force. Later, they join Jamil and his Vulture crew in a grueling adventure aimed at   protecting the last of the remaining Newtypes and bringing genuine peace to mankind. ➜

GUNDAM X
MOBILE SUIT : GX-9900 ガンダムエックス

The Gundam Legacy

With writer/director Shinji Takamatsu at the helm, *Gundam X* attempts to combine the best of the UC Gundam saga and *Gundam Wing*. The introduction of Newtypes is explored for the first time in an alternate-universe Gundam series. *Gundam X's* mechas were designed by the familiar duo of Kunio Okawara and Junya Ishigaki, who worked together in *V Gundam* and *Gundam Wing*. Here, most of the mobile suits have the unmistakable UC Gundam look mixed with a strong touch of festive/expressive elements common to *Gundam Wing's* mecha design.

Gundam X features the artful orchestral soundtracks of composer Yasuo Higuchi, plus highly listenable J-pop and R&B-oriented opening and ending themes.

The imperfect character designs and executed scripts take away from the positives, however. As with *Gundam 0083*, *X* features a bunch of wide-eyed, but less-than-interesting personalities: Garrod Ran will forever be remembered as a pale imitation of Judeau Ashta from *Gundam*

ZZ, while the sad-faced, dreary-eyed Tiffa Adill lacks the fire and intrigue of previous Gundam characters. The blame rests squarely on Takamatsu, who turns a potentially engrossing story into a never-ending journey across a post-war wasteland.

Unsurprisingly, the series was cut short to three-quarters of its planned length (39 episodes instead of 52). *Gundam X*, for all its good intentions, reminds us that not everything with *Gundam* in its title is successful.

Mobile Suit Gundam – The 08th MS Team: OVA

Miller's Report – motion picture

The 08th MS Team is the latest One Year War-related Gundam saga. It's also the longest-running Gundam saga (three-and-a-half years, from 1996 to 1999, for the 12 episodes).

The timeline's set in October UC 0079. The focus is on Shiroh Amada, a

23-year-old Federal Force officer dispatched from his native Side-2 space colony to the vicious battlefield on Earth and assigned to lead a newly organized mobile-suit team to fight the Zeon Forces in the war-hardened Southeast Asian frontline. Armed with profound mechanical knowledge and a hatred of Zeon's brutality, Shiroh quickly wins the trust and loyalty of his fellow teammates. His unyielding faith, however, is put to the test when he meets and falls in love with Aina Sakhalin. The female Zeon test pilot is entrusted by her engineer brother with the job of testing a secret weapon of mass destruction, which would drastically alter the war's outcome.

Faced with the choice of loving one's enemy and fighting for freedom, Shiroh makes a fateful decision. As the Federal Force closes in, Zeon's secret weapon enters into its final phase. Now nothing can prepare Shiroh and his loyal teammates for what's ahead. ➡

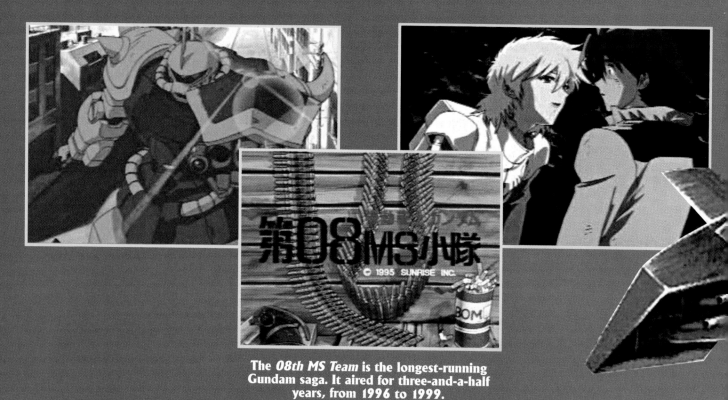

The *08th MS Team* is the longest-running Gundam saga. It aired for three-and-a-half years, from 1996 to 1999.

The 12-episode series delivers a a well-written, adult-oriented storyline that doesn't mess around.

21

2

Gundam Wing

The Gundam Legacy

Director Mitsuko Kase did a smart thing by adding a new character (Alice Miller) to spice up the previously seen stories. New footage clarifies events from the OVA without spoiling what's been told. The story is told through the eyes of Miller, an intelligence officer dispatched by the Federal Force's military court to investigate a spying allegation leveled against Shiroh Amada (because of his encounter with Aina). The movie focuses on Tomino's core themes of war and peace and moral uncertainty.

Miller's Report is a concise version of the OVA, with merits of its own. There's no fancy, over-the-top MS fighting scenes here, just the right dose of human interaction and food for thought.

New Mobile Report Gundam Wing: Endless Waltz – OVA and motion picture

The abrupt and somewhat mystifying conclusion of the *Gundam Wing* TV series in March 1996 left many fans confused, but it couldn't dampen their desire for more from the ever-popular group of five teenage Gundam pilots. Their prayers were answered 10 months later, when the *Endless Waltz* sequel was released in early 1997.

A three-episode OVA, *Endless Waltz* (which was later retooled into a 90-minute motion picture or Gundam's 20th-anniversary celebration) picks up where the *Gundam Wing* left off. One year after the grueling conflicts ended between the space colonists and the Earth Sphere Alliance, the warring factions made their peace and united under the single entity Earth Sphere United Nation.

The peace ended abruptly when a mysterious armed force known as the Mariemaia Army launched a sudden, all-out assault on the ESUN's headquarters →

The 08th features a well-written, adult-oriented storyline that doesn't mess around. Robo-show-veteran director Takeyuki Kanda presents the One Year War in a real-life, militaristic manner that many long-time UC Gundam fans will find instantly attractive. Character designer Toshihiro Kawamoto deserves a thumbs-up for his cast of multi-faceted characters.

The anticipated slump in the series' quality never materialized after Kanda's sudden passing in 1996. Instead, the direction taken by new director Umanosuke Iida turned out to be a blessing, with more classic OYW mechas and one-on-one MS battles being featured in the second half of the series.

Mecha-wise, *The 08th* showcases the incomparable design trio of Kunio Okawara (*0079*), Hajime Katoki (*0083*) and Kimitoshi Yamane (*G Gundam*). Their realistic new Gundam design, plus their excellent reworking of some of the long-

forgotten MS from the *0079* era, have been justified by the ever-growing popularity of Bandai's *08* model series. The show is also complemented by Kohei Tanaka's strong, atmospheric background music and by the punchy theme songs performed by Chihiro Yonekura.

Still, the most attractive aspect of *08* is its lively and tasteful treatment of characters. Witness the relationship between Shiroh and Aina, the camaraderie between the 08th MS Team members, and most of all, Shiroh and Aina's public declaration of their views on war and humanity. The message that there's always hope if you try, set against the grim and cruel backdrop of One Year War, makes this a gripping and enjoyable series – the best Gundam OVA since *0080*.

To cash in on *08*'s success and celebrate Gundam's 20th birthday in 1999, Sunrise Japan unleashed Miller's Report, a 50-minute movie that summarizes the first half of the OVA.

and held its leader, Relena Peacecraft, hostage. Turns out the attack was Operation Meteor, carefully planned by Dakim Barton, the powerful and cunning patriarch of the Barton Group, which financed the first Operation Meteor against the Earth Sphere Alliance in AC 195.

By installing the young daughter of the late OZ leader Treize Kushrenada as its figurehead, Dakim hoped to ensure his domination of the newly born Earth-space nation. Sensing their former backer was up to no good, the Gundam pilots, along with the ESUN's special task force, the Preventer Agency, acted swiftly against the Mariemaia Army. With only a handful of war-hardened ace pilots standing against a tidal wave of well-trained and well-equipped invaders, could the heroes of the last war pull off another miracle in the pursuit of everlasting peace?

Endless Waltz is a genuine surprise in many ways. Not only is it the sequel to *Gundam Wing*, it's also a prequel to the popular TV series that dwells on the mysterious past of the five Gundam pilots and their relationships with their mentors – the five scientists who created the ultimate weapons.

All the featured mechas received a sparkling new redesign, courtesy of superstar designer Hajime Katoki. The real joy however, is to witness the maturing of the five Gundam pilots who have a true leader (Quatre) and an embittered outcast (Wu-Fei). While the show's character design and setting continues to be beautiful, *Endless Waltz* has finally shed the accusations about *Gundam Wing* being five pretty boys piloting killing machines.

Endless Waltz's strong showing has proven once and for all that experimental Gundam stories can be every bit as good as the traditional UC Gundam saga. Don't miss *Endless Waltz.*

Turn-A is set in the year 2345 of a new calendar – 2,000 years after the dawn of the Space Age.

Turn-A pits Gundam vs. Gundam in a spectacular battle for universal supremacy.

Turn-A Gundam: TV series

When Yoshiyuki Tomino, creator of the original Gundam series and many of its successors, announced his return with a new Gundam TV series in time for Gundam's 20th anniversary in 1999, fans who longed for the good old days of the early '80s had high hopes. But when the final design was revealed, fans all over the world were shocked. *Turn-A Gundam* looked like

anything but the kind of designs they were hoping for. Endless whispers about Tomino's declining creativity and his attitude towards Gundam made the rounds.

Now, roughly six months after the conclusion of the *Turn-A* TV series in Japan, all the negative rumors about Tomino's wisdom and Gundam's future have been swept away. *Turn-A* has once again proven that Tomino can create epic and ➡

The Gundam Legacy

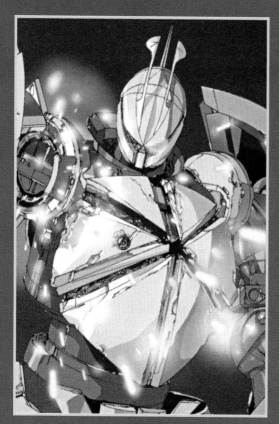

memorable Gundam sagas, and his love of Gundam has never been stronger.

Running at a marathon 50 episodes between 1999 and 2000, *Turn-A* tells the story of Loran Seack, a 15-year-old youngster who was among those selected by the Lunar settlers Moonrace to explore the possibility of living on planet Earth. The time is the year 2345 of a new calendar, 2,000 years after the dawn of the Space Age. After centuries of war, chaos, and peace, the people on Earth have lost the technology they once possessed and forgotten that they once traveled in space.

The Moonrace has retained all those technologies, and now they regard the planet that they once left behind with envious eyes. Hoping for a better life on Earth, the Moonrace, led by their queen and spiritual leader Diana Soleil, descend onto Earth in the year 2347 and try to obtain a huge portion of the planet's territory from the planet's feudal leaders for their eventual immigration. Unable to

strike a deal with the Earth's feudal lords, the hawkish faction of the Moonrace decides to seize the Earth's territory by force, and the Earth people responded by swiftly forming local militias armed with only outdated technology to stand against Moonrace's advanced mobile suits.

Loran, now 17 years old and having developed a strong affection for the living planet and its people, can no longer stand aside as the conflict engulfs his home. One day he discovers an unusual relic – an ancient mobile suit entombed in stone, ignored by the locals for ages. Loran's destiny is changed forever when he becomes the pilot of this powerful machine – known as "Gundam" by the Moonrace and regarded with fear and respect – joins the Earth's militia and fights against his own race to protect his beloved new homeland.

As the conflict enters a critical phase and peace seems to have been stolen by opportunists on both sides, mankind is shocked by the sudden revelation of the "Black History" – the darkest chapters of a long-forgotten human civilization in which the true identity of Loran's Gundam and its relation to the human race's glorious past are also revealed. Could this moment of truth, coupled with the efforts of Loran and his allies, finally bring peace to the Earth and the Moon?

As the top feature of Gundam's 20th-anniversary "Big Bang Project," Tomino and Nippon Sunrise spared no expense in enlisting some of animation's big names in today's animation industry to enhance "Turn-A." This includes character designer Akira Yasuda (Capcom's *Street Fighter II*); the mecha design quartet of Kunio Okawara, Syd Mead, Atsushi Shigeta and Takumi Sakura; art director Shigemi Ikeda; and composer Yoko Kanno (*Macross Plus,*

Cowboy Bebop, Escaflowne).

With a top-quality production staff at his disposal, Tomino presents his latest version of the Gundam universe, which looks nothing like any of the previous Gundam universes, yet becomes strangely familiar upon closer examination. Viewers will recognize the show's pan-European setting is similar to the setting of *Char's Counterattack* 12 years ago.

The series also deals in folklores and myths, a fixture of every Tomino-penned Gundam series. And its new timeline seems to suggest another alternate-universe Gundam series. In fact, the *Turn-A* title represents a logical symbol called the "universal quantifier," which means "all the elements of a set."

Turn-A is intended to encompass all the Gundam sagas from the last two decades, including the alternate-universe series. As evidence, note the gradual appearances of mobile suits, mechas and technology from the UC era and alternate universes. Syd Mead's design of *Turn-A Gundam* has been hotly debated, and it's true that *Turn-A* has a radical design some fans may find difficult to accept. Once the storyline gets you, though, fans will find Mead's designs fit in nicely with the tone of the show.

Tomino smartly took a page out of the faulty *0083* series and turned it into a spectacular sequence of Gundam vs. Gundam: the final battle between the encompassing *Turn-A* and the mighty and menacing *Turn-X*. The outcome is so surprising that one can only marvel at the genius of Tomino the originator. Ignore all the unfair comments about Tomino and *Turn-A Gundam*. Watch the show and be your own judge. You won't be disappointed.

Now you can understand why Gundam is so revered by fans worldwide. If you want to learn more about the Gundam saga on the Internet, here are some great Gundam sites to try: ➜

Roughly six months after the conclusion of the *Turn-A* series in Japan, the excitement is hardly winding down.

The Gundam Legacy

Official Sites:

Bandai Entertainment (http://www.bandai-ent.com/): Responsible for launching the Gundam Wing TV series in the USA.

GundamOfficial.com (http://GundamOfficial.com/): Launched by Bandai America and Anime Village, it covers the Gundam Wing TV series and includes story summaries and product information.

Gundam Perfect Web (http://www.gundam.channel.or.jp/): A Japanese-language site launched by Bandai Japan, with detailed information on the latest Gundam model releases, merchandise and events.

Nippon Sunrise (http://www.nifty.ne.jp/station/sunrise/): The company that creates and owns all the Gundam series.

Sunrise Interactive (http://www.atsai.co.jp/~sun/top.htm): Has the latest news on Gundam-related video games and multimedia.

Anime Village (http://www.animevillage.com/): The company that introduced Gundam to North American fans. You can order Gundam videos there, or chat with Gundam fans on the Internet.

Fan Sites:

Pojo's Gundam Web (www.pojo.com/gundam): Coming soon.

Gundam Project (http://www.gundamproject.com/): The most informative Gundam fan site on the Net. Useful features include story synopses and historical and technological articles, plus domestic and imported merchandise information.

Gundam.com (http://www.gundam.com/): Features comprehensive character and mobile suit databases, a fan arts gallery, interactive sections and more.

Its Side-7 Colony (http://www.gundam.com/side7/): The home of many fine Gundam fan sites.

Newtype Asylum (http://www.gundam.com/side7/newtype_asylum/): Features Gundam model reviews, introductions of Gundam mechas and characters, news, articles and reviews on Gundam animation series, music, books, merchandise and more.

Mecha Domain (http://mechadomain.gundam.com/): A one-stop online reference database of all Gundam MS, ships and other mechas, including statistics and high-quality images of all the known variants.

The Shinigami Project (http://www.shinigami.org/): Features analyses of Gundam Wing's mechas and characters, plus Wing-related articles and FAQs.

The Gundam Mailing List (GML) (http://gundam.aeug.org/): If you have any question about Gundam, it'll be answered here. You'll hear opinions from all walks of life, from experts to newcomers. You can subscribe to the GML or simply read through the monthly archives that are constantly updated.

Gundam Wing Mailing Lists (GWMLs) (http://www.gundamwing.org/ml/): Descriptions of and membership information for the five Wing-related mailing lists hosted by Gundam Wing International. ∎

www.gundamproject.com

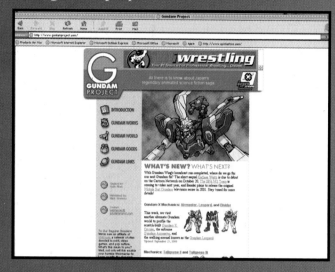

www.gundam.com

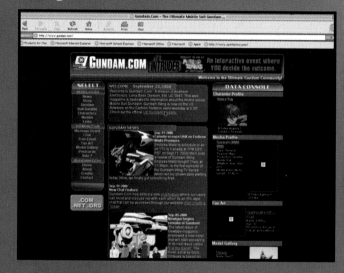

wingzero.net

The Third Dimension

G-Force

Gundam Wing is the latest – and maybe the greatest – force in anime

By Hal Hintze

What's the hottest anime of summer 2000? Place your bet on Gundam Wing, the Cartoon Network's snowballing sci-fi hit.

With characters that are as deep as Pokémon and action scenes to rival that of Dragon Ball Z, the futuristic Gundam Wing continues to grab fans by the millions. Already G-Wing has reached the No. 8 position on leading Web portal Lycos' list of hot search topics, and it'll likely be higher by the time you finish reading this.

What makes Gundamania so interesting? There's actually several Gundams with vastly different plot lines and concepts, each with tangled characters and story lines inside every series. Though all of it –

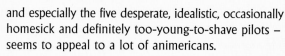

and especially the five desperate, idealistic, occasionally homesick and definitely too-young-to-shave pilots – seems to appeal to a lot of animericans.

Gundam Wing the Cartoon Series

Cartoon, cartoon, indeed! The surge in Gundamania starts with Gundam Wing's appearance as part of the Cartoon Network's Toonami package.

Since March, two slightly different versions of this classic Japanese series – sometimes called "Mobile Suit Gundam Wing" over in the states and originally known in Japan by a third name, "Gundam W" – have gathered a vast amount of fans on this side of the big pond.

G-Force

While both of Cartoon Network's versions of G-Wing are faithful translations of the original, the late-afternoon version is slightly edited to remove an occasional violent scene or two. The late-night version, translated but otherwise unedited from the Japanese original, restores even the wildest action sequences to the mix.

Don't fret if your folks won't let you stay up for the late-night version; you're not missing much.

What's neat about Gundam Wing is the complexity of the characters, the continual weaving and reweaving of the plot and the pile of realism it delivers that's sorely missing from most other anime. But with all this complexity, it helps if you know where to start.

Here's the basic plot set-up: It's the year After Colony (AC) 195, a time when space colonies exist to ease Earth's population pressures. It's also a time of severe political repression; violent wars have left Earth under the control of an evil government called the United Earth Sphere Alliance. The alliance, which comes complete with its secret military society (OZ) and its behind-the-scenes corporate force (the Romefeller Foundation), is extending its iron-fisted control into space, seeking to eliminate all opposition, even in the freedom-loving space colonies.

One of the principal means of force is the mobile suit, a giant, human-shaped battle machine with a pilot inside. Typically, mobile suits are hundreds of feet tall and capable of space flight. Each also carries immense firepower.

After decades of losing ground, scientists from the space colonies devise a last-ditch plan: the development of five superior mobile suits, called Gundams, to battle the Earth Alliance forces. The Gundams, so named because they make use of a superior metal alloy called Gundanium, are to be sent to Earth to battle the Alliance's own machines.

Five young men, each only 15 years of age, are chosen to pilot the Gundam suits. Each colony's team of scientists supplies one of the Gundam suits, along with its pilot. Each suit has its own design and capabilities. The plot, called "Operation Meteor," calls for the pilots to bring the suits to Earth in secrecy and work independently of each other, causing as much damage and wreaking as

GUNDAM ON TV

Here's a listing of Japanese Gundam TV/movie releases to date, along with number of episodes and original airing dates. Note that this does not include compilations such as the *Mobile Suit Gundam I/II/III* movies, which were extracted from the original series.

Gundam Saga (Universal Century timeline):

Mobile Suit Gundam
(TV, 49 episodes, 1979-80)
Mobile Suit Z Gundam
(TV, 50 episodes, 1985-86)
Mobile Suit Gundam ZZ
(TV, 46 episodes, 1986-87)
Mobile Suit Gundam: Char's Counterattack (Movie, 1988)
Mobile Suit Gundam 0080: War in the Pocket
(TV, 6 episodes, 1989)
Mobile Suit Gundam F-91
(Movie, 1991)
Mobile Suit Gundam 0083: Stardust Memory
(TV, 13 episodes, 1991)

Mobile Suit V Gundam
(TV, 52 episodes, 1993-94)
Mobile Suit Gundam: The 08th MS Team (TV, 13 episodes, 1996)

Alternate Universes (After Colony timeline):

New Mobile Report Gundam W
(U.S.: Gundam Wing)
(TV, 49 episodes,1995-96)
New Mobile Report Gundam W: Endless Waltz
(TV, three episodes, 1997)

(Future Century timeline):

Mobile Fighter G Gundam
(TV, 49 episodes. 1994-95)

(After War timeline):

After War: Gundam X
(TV, 39 episodes, 1996)
Also:
Turn A Gundam (TV, 51 episodes, presently airing in Japan)

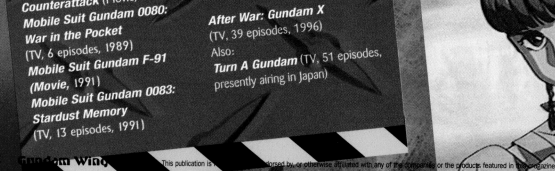

much havoc as possible. But of course, things never go exactly to plan.

The 49 G-Wing episodes detail plot twist after plot twist as the young characters learn more about themselves and the forces that steer them. Each of the young, idealistic pilots have weak spots, and several have hidden secrets that we learn about through the series. The pilots aren't always good, and on the other side, the bad guys aren't always bad.

One of the most interesting characters is the mysterious Zechs Merquise, a 19-year-old pilot who has quickly advanced within the Earth Alliance and OZ. Only problem is that Merquise's own goals may not be those of either OZ or the Alliance. There's also the beautiful Relena Darlian, OZ heavyweights Treize Khushrenada and Lady Une, the scientists who designed and built the suits, business and government leaders, and dozens of other minor characters whom you will come to know through the course of the show. There's intrigue aplenty, and enough boy-meets-girl to keep that interesting, too.

But back to the Gundam pilots. After all, they're the stars of the show. The five pilots are:

• **Heero Yuy:** Pilot, Wing Gundam (also known as Gundam 01, the suit launched from the "L1" space-colony cluster). Heero, the show's most important character, is the ultimate mobile-suit pilot. His suit, the eponymous Wing Gundam, was designed and built by Doctor J – no, not the basketball player – and is so named because it can transform into "bird mode," allowing it to fly and even enter Earth's atmosphere from outer space. (The other Gundam suits, though capable of fighting in outer space, are not designed for winged flight, meaning they mostly battle on the ground while they're on Earth.) Heero is detached and reserved, a ruthless machine who's been trained since childhood for this mission. He's not really Heero, but is instead a nameless waif who was re-named after the original Heero Yuy, a leader of the space colonies who was assassinated in AC 175. Heero also goes on to master the "Zero System," part of an advanced form of the Wing Gundam that...whoops! Don't want to give away too much of the story.

• **Duo Maxwell:** Pilot, Gundam Deathscythe (Gundam 02, from the L2 colony cluster). Duo's the natural counterbalance to the overly serious Heero, a lighthearted, outward-going sort who still maintains control during battle. Duo, the most religious of the Gundam pilots, grew up a street urchin in the L2 colonies and became part of the Sweeper Group, a space-salvaging operation. His suit, the Deathscythe, was designed by the Sweeper Group's Professor G, an expert in stealth technology. The suit features radar jammers and a weapon called a beam scythe, which makes short work of the enemy's mobile suits.

• **Trowa Barton:** Pilot, Gundam Heavyarms (Gundam 03, from the L3 colony cluster). The young pilot called Trowa Barton is an even greater mystery than Heero Yuy. Like Heero, he's reserved and detached, but where Heero is machine-like, Trowa is calm and quiet. Trowa is a trained acrobat; the skills are also of great use to him at the controls of his Gundam. Trowa's suit comes from the L3 cluster and is the brainchild of that colony's Doctor S. The Heavyarms suit speaks for itself, carrying far more raw firepower than any of the other Gundam suits.

• **Quatre Raberba Winner:** Gundam Sandrock (Gundam 04, from the L4 colony cluster). Quatre comes from the Winner family, the ultra-rich, civically responsible leaders of the L4 colonies. Quatre's family resources, as secretly used by Instructor H, fund the development of the Sandrock suit. Quatre is a test-tube baby, the 30th child and the only son of his wealthy, peace-loving father. (Can you imagine having 29 older sisters? Sheeesh!) Quatre goes against his father's beliefs in training for the Gundam Sandrock, setting up a painful conflict. This is due to the fact that where Quatre's father decries violence at all costs, Quatre detests the bloodshed but will do what he has to do to save his people.

→

• **Chang Wufei:** Pilot, Shenlong Gundam (Gundam 05, from the L5 colony cluster) Wufei comes from an ancient Chinese warrior clan, exiled decades earlier to the L5 colonies by an unjust government. Wufei's suit, the Shenlong Gundam, was developed by Master O using the resources of Wufei's clan – Shenlong means "God Dragon" in Chinese – and Wufei pilots the Shenlong Gundam with the pride and honor that his upbringing demands. Wufei's code of honor has infused his character with a rigidity that sometimes leads him to make difficult choices, though Wufei invariably comes down on the side of good.

Gundam Appeal

So now you know the main players, but you still haven't been provided with a reason why you should care about Gundam Wing. Here it is: Gundam Wing is simply better than most of the anime of the recent Japanese invasion. Sure, like the majority of other cartoons, Gundam Wing is a pastiche of tried-and-true cartoon elements – fast-paced action, pretty-boy lead characters designed to appeal to boys and girls, and tons of high-tech gizmos just waiting to be made into play-action toys and models.

But G-Wing is a better pastiche than most of its competition.

Particularly with Japanese cartoons, this designed-to-sell-toys idea has been a part of the deal for decades. The development of the original Gundam series, in fact, was funded by a couple of Japanese die-cast toy makers, then acquired by Bandai soon after. But Gundam is only one of several dozen properties to follow this path, from Ronin Warriors to Mighty Morphin Power Rangers to Transformers – a knockoff of a knockoff of an idea if there ever was one.

Gundam Wing succeeds where most of its rivals fail because of the depth and complexity of its characters. You'll enjoy discovering some of the secrets behind the mysterious Trowa Barton, anguish with Quatre Raberba Winner when OZ takes over his father's colony and forces his father into a no-win predicament and go "A-ha! So that's the connection!" when another piece of the plot unfolds. Of all the recent Japanese arrivals, only Pokémon rivals Gundam Wing in this regard: In both series, the lead characters are mature, making mistakes and learning from them.

And Gundam Wing is illustrated well, using the lush shojo (girls') manga style. Backgrounds and colors are rich, and unlike, say, Dragon Ball Z, you're spared the endless moments of

characters lying on the ground, shaking and groaning (This practice is the Japanese variation of the characters in Hanna-Barbera cartoons running in place against a moving-but-repeating background. It eats up time and saves bucks in the animation process. Ugh.).

The drawback? Gundam Wing can be a tough nut to crack. The characters' complexity and the plot twists make it extremely difficult to watch a single episode and understand what's going on.

PW

Endless Waltz

A conclusion to the Gundam Wing saga that is both a prequel, because of its explanatory flashbacks, and a sequel.

Mobile Suit

A humanoid machine standing more than fifty feet tall which is operated by a human pilot. Different types of mobile suits are designed for land, sea, air or space combat.

Operation Meteor

A rebel group's plan to liberate the colonies from the earth's control using five advanced mobile suits called Gundams.

OZ

A secret society created by the Romefeller Foundation, which plots to infiltrate the Alliance and take control of Earth. The leader of OZ is Treize Kushrenada.

Romefeller Foundation

A powerful arms manufacturer that develops and provides the Alliance with mobile suits. Their influence over the Alliance leads to the cruel oppression of the conquered colonies.

Sanc Kingdom

A small European nation dedicated to pacifism that was wiped out by the Earth Alliance 13 years ago. Its ruler, King Peacecraft, was killed and his children Miliardo and Relena disappeared.

Space Colonies

Huge wheel-shaped space stations in Earth orbit, which house millions of people. The space colonies are grouped into clusters at five gravitationally stable positions around the Earth. These colonies are strictly controlled by the Earth Alliance and yearn for independence.

Specials

An elite branch of the Earth Alliance military, staffed and trained by the Romefeller Foundation, which specializes in mobile suit combat. It serves as a cover for OZ's infiltration of the Alliance command structure.

United Earth Sphere Alliance

The organization that governs both Earth and the space colonies. Often referred to as the Earth Alliance, or simply the Alliance. Though created to unite the world and maintain peace, the Alliance is a military organization that rules through force.

The Politics of Gundam Wing

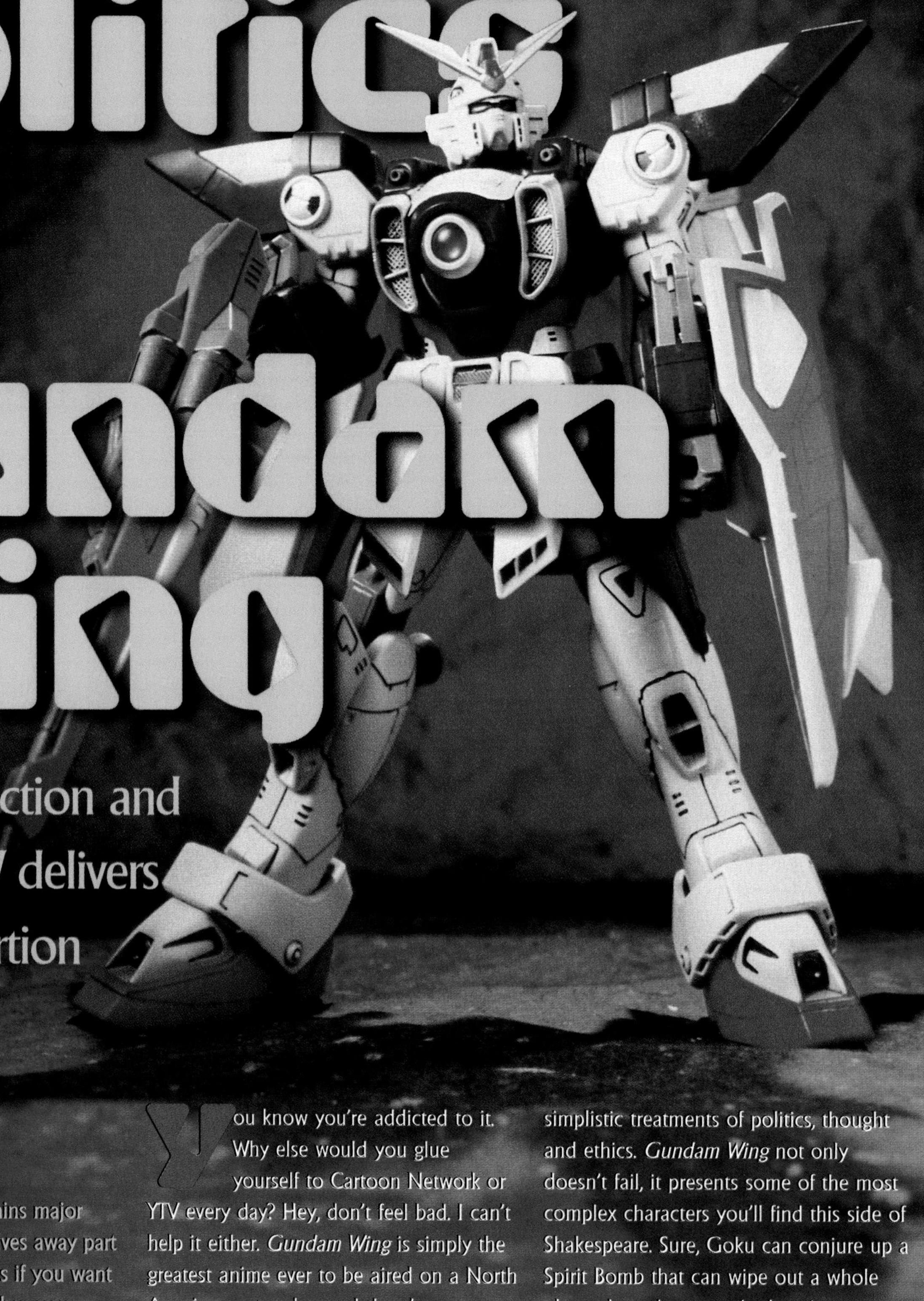

Along with action and
violence, GW delivers
a healthy portion
of thought

By Bryan Gividen

WARNING: This article contains major spoilers – information that gives away part of the series! Do not read this if you want to be completely surprised when you watch Endless Waltz.

ou know you're addicted to it. Why else would you glue yourself to Cartoon Network or YTV every day? Hey, don't feel bad. I can't help it either. *Gundam Wing* is simply the greatest anime ever to be aired on a North American network – and there's a reason. Most other anime series fail in their

simplistic treatments of politics, thought and ethics. *Gundam Wing* not only doesn't fail, it presents some of the most complex characters you'll find this side of Shakespeare. Sure, Goku can conjure up a Spirit Bomb that can wipe out a whole planet, but when was the last time you saw Goku try to impose justice – true justice, not revenge – upon his opponents? And when is the last time our boy Tenchi tried committing suicide so that his mission wouldn't fail?

If you want to know where all this great stuff comes from, you absolutely have to watch *Endless Waltz*. One event caused the Gundams to fall to Earth to wreak their havoc, and it's about as despicable as an event can get. A few minor details are revealed near the end of the *Gundam Wing* series, but not enough to understand the real political reasons behind that most horrible event – Operation Meteor.

Operation Meteor

When we're first told about Operation Meteor, it appears to be a straightforward guerrilla mission with the Gundam pilots going to Earth to do a few hit-and-run attacks on the ruling, semi-evil Earth Sphere Alliance and its secret organization, OZ.

While it sounds like the Gundams were at least on the side of right in this operation, their original purpose was far less than heroic.

Operation Meteor was actually the brainchild of Dekim Barton, whose plans were to:

1) Drop a floating Colony or two onto the Earth, causing worldwide destruction and panic;

2) Send the Gundams to Earth to rough up everyone and render all military defenses useless;

3) Overthrow the Earth Nation, unifying the Earth and the Colonies.

Good plan, eh? And it was – until everyone's ethics got in the way. Every one of the Gundam Scientists who trained a young pilot knew that this act would cause much grief and pain, so they changed the plan. (Note: The irony of Dekim's plan to drop colonies on the Earth was that Zechs, who had completely different goals than Dekim, was going to drop the Battleship Libra and Peacemillion on Earth, which also would have allowed Dekim to step in and take the glory – and the throne.)

Instead of following Dekim's plans for global domination, the Gundam pilots took off to destroy OZ instead – a little less terrifying and ambitious than what Dekim had in mind. We see the leader of the White Fang become wildly upset with the Gundam Scientists for "changing the plan." Of all the events in *Gundam Wing*, Operation Meteor is the most devious.

Peace Through War

Another example of the philosophical content of *Gundam Wing* can be seen in comparing the Peacecraft children, Relena and Zechs/Milliardo. Polar opposites, right? Maybe not.

Think of the Peacecrafts as different paths to a final destination – a long route full of twists and turns, and a short, messy route blasted through any opposition – and they seem a lot more alike than different.

Relena traveled the first road. She knew complete pacifism would be a harder course to follow, but she knew that if she could do it her way, many lives would be spared. Total pacifism would mean peace in the end, but it was a much more complex and difficult route to follow because there were so many people with goals of their own that got in her way.

Milliardo, on the other hand, felt that peace could never be achieved by just watching the wars pass by. Instead, Milliardo constructed a brilliant yet

controversial plan: he would show the world just how destructive war was, and then no one would want to fight. And what better way to do that than by staging a "grand war," as Dorothy Catalina put it? By fighting and destroying as many lives as possible, Milliardo would force people to recognize the horrors of war – an ingenious, selfish, horrible plan.

The Connections

Gundam Wing is supposed to have a lot of World War II inferences. You see this through the mass murders, the expressions of superiority, the clothing, the names and more (the Zero was a deadly Japanese fighter plane in WWII... is this where the ZERO system came from?) Other Gundam series are even more explicit with their WWII references. But when you consider that the first Gundam series aired a little more than 30 years after the war's end, why wouldn't Gundam have WWII overtones? It's actually amazing that there are no references to Hitler or concentration camps.

These influences and overtones make the series all the more vibrant and engaging. The detailed storylines, from the irony of the Gundam Scientists fixing what they've done to the effects of the ZERO system on Quatre, even the ethical catfights between Dorothy and Relena, make for great viewing. Now only if so many Gundams hadn't joined the "destroyed" list. ■

The Gundam Files

Vital stats and bios on all the key characters

Quatre Raberba Winner

Gundam Pilots

Quatre Raberba Winner

Mobile Suit: Gundam Sandrock
Age: 15
Sex: Male
Ethnicity: Arab
Origin: Colony LaGrange Point 4
Family: Sisters (29), Father (1), Mother (1 - deceased)
Height: 156 cm
Weight: 41 kg
Eye Color: Blue-green
Hair Color: Blond

Quatre Raberba Winner not only has the hardest name to spell but is the gentlest of all the pilots. Quatre's history is a unique one. For one thing, he has 29 sisters, all of whom are test-tube children who grew and developed in artificial wombs. (The reason for so many test-tube children, as explained in the *Gundam Wing Manga*, is that the movement to space affected many pregnancies). Quatre is the only child in his family to have been the result of a natural birth, but his mother died while giving birth to him. Seeing no reason to make Quatre feel any different from his sisters, his father told Quatre that he was a test-tube baby. Quatre grew up feeling like an experiment and eventually grew to resent his life and felt he had no purpose.

This all changed when a space carrier he was on was hijacked by a group of space pirates called the Maganac Corps. Quatre found out all of the Maganacs were test-tube babies. In fact, they were very proud of that fact. He joined their ranks and developed his own sense of self respect and pride. Quatre later ferreted out a traitor among the Maganacs, helped them fight off the Federation and risked his life for them. Two years later, when Operation Meteor was launched, Quatre met up with them again.

From that time on, Quatre looked at every life as a valuable one, never letting himself believe he was any better or any less a person than anyone else. Quatre makes sure every single one of his enemies has a chance to repent and surrender before he attacks them (and usually apologizes after killing them as well!). Quatre would love to be a pacifist, but he knows that only through fighting the enemy can the war be won.

The Gundam Sandrock is Quatre's, although at one point Quatre found the plans for the Wing ZERO (which Professor H left in the Winner Family computers), had it built and went on a rampage with it. Quatre wanted the Wing ZERO to avenge his father's death at the hands of colony soldiers, so he took it upon himself to blow up each colony one at a time. His rampage of destruction was only stopped when, under the orders of OZ, Heero and Trowa teamed up and used Mercurius and Vayeate to defeat Quatre.

Despite that rare outburst, Quatre held the other pilots down to earth by using his quiet voice to talk of peace.

Heero Yuy

Mobile Suit: Gundam Wing
Age: 15
Sex: Male
Ethnicity: Japanese
Origin: Colony LaGrange Point 1
Family: Unknown
Height: 156 cm
Weight: 45 kg
Eye Color: Blue
Hair Color: Brown

Only two things are known for certain about Heero Yuy, the "perfect soldier" of

Heero Yuy

the Gundam Wing saga: 1) his real name isn't "Heero Yuy," and 2) we don't know what his real name is.

Sent from Colony LaGrange Point 1 and trained by the huge-glasses-wearing, metal-armed, eccentric Dr. J., Heero is the most silent and deadly warrior among the five Gundam pilots. While it's said that nothing can stop Heero from fulfilling his mission, throughout the series he is distracted by his emotions. (But then, sweet, beautiful princesses from fallen kingdoms have that effect on most guys.)

Besides the romance that developed between Heero and Relena, Heero developed a special connection with Trowa. The quiet pair teamed up several times during various parts of the series, and every time it made a great

partnership. Both have a "total-war" attitude and the willingness to sacrifice themselves and anything else to make sure their job gets done.

Heero's Mobile Suit piloting skills are among the best around. Heero piloted many different Mobile Suits in the series, but the two he used most regularly were Gundam Wing and Wing ZERO. Heero was sent to Earth using the Gundam Wing, and on multiple occasions he tried to destroy his Gundam to prevent others from gaining it. In the 10th episode, when he faced off against Zechs Merquise, Heero finally had no choice but to use the self-destruct button to prevent Lady Une from destroying the colonies. Later in the series, Wing ZERO and Heero became like one. The two really were meant for each ➡

The Gundam Files

other. Heero is one of the few pilots who could actually tame the ZERO system, and that shows just how good a pilot he is.

In the end not much more is revealed about Heero than was known in the beginning. However, he did come out of his shell and open up to various people along the way, especially Relena.

As for Heero's role in Endless Waltz, he's the key to the whole series. We don't want to reveal too much, but we will say that Heero's cool head and deadpan one-liners, mixed with his let-it-all-hang-out battle style, will captivate you.

Duo Maxwell

Mobile Suit: Gundam Deathscythe
Age: 15
Sex: Male
Ethnicity: American
Origin: Colony LaGrange Point 2
Family: Unknown
Height: 156 cm
Weight: 43 kg
Eye Color: Blue
Hair Color: Brown

Duo Maxwell, "The God of Death," Shinigami. Call him whatever you like; he is by far the deadliest of the Mobile Suit pilots. We know more about Duo's past than the other pilots. Duo was one of the many children left to fend for himself after the war killed his parents. He and other orphans scrounged the streets of their colony looking for food, and they

Duo Maxwell

got it any way possible. While he was eventually caught, he was taken in by the priest of a church called the Maxwell Church. There, Duo cleaned up his life (which helps explain why he dresses like a minister throughout Gundam Wing). Duo's hair was first braided by his favorite nun at the Maxwell Church. When asked about his hairstyle by the other characters, Duo said, "It made it easier to steal and not get caught." He kept the hair ever since.

Eventually, the war returned to Duo's colony. Soldiers stormed the Maxwell Church and demanded things from the priest. Overhearing the soldiers talking about needing a mobile suit, Duo told them he would retrieve one for them. By

dodging military defenses at a local base, Duo was able to steal a suit. But when he returned to Maxwell Street, he found the church completely destroyed, the priest dead and the nun dying. With her last words, she told Duo that the father kept peace in his heart and Duo in his mind until the very end.

Duo had seen his parents die, and now his surrogate family was dead, too. From that time forward, he used the name "Shinigami," which in Japanese religions means, "The God of Death."

Eventually, Duo met up with Professor G, the long-nosed, bowl-cut-wearing scientist. Professor G designed the Deathscythe Gundam for close and quick combat, and he optimized the machine for Duo because of Duo's miraculous piloting skills. Later in the series when OZ troops captured Duo's Deathscythe, they made an example of it and broadcast its destruction live via satellite. Duo is also captured soon after, along with Professor G, Wufei and Heero. Professor G began construction on an upgraded version of Deathscythe, which he cleverly named "Deathscythe Hell."

Chang Wufei

Mobile Suit: Gundam Shenlong, Gundam Altlong
Age: 15
Sex: Male
Ethnicity: Chinese
Origin: Colony LaGrange Point 5
Family: Merian (wife - deceased)
Height: 156 cm
Weight: 46 kg
Eye Color: Black
Hair Color: Black

Chang Wufei (more commonly called "Wufei") is the self-appointed judge, jury and executioner of the Gundam pilots' enemies. Wufei takes it upon himself to determine who is and isn't worthy of life. Heavy burden, eh? There are no shades of gray for Wufei; he sees everything in stark black and white.

Wufei's hyperactive sense of justice is rooted in his clan's history. He was born into a dynasty of warriors who believed in self-discipline, honor and defending the weak. The Dragon clan was a very powerful and respected clan in Eurasia until people began to fear its power. Wufei's clan was forced out of China and into a space colony. This

event was forever etched into his mind, and it poured out through his guns.

For example, when he discovered the evil intentions of some of those involved in Operation Meteor, he stormed away, taking his beloved Gundam Shenlong (which he calls "Nataku") with him, but not before vowing to kill all those who stood in the way of what he felt was right.

Wufei uses the Mobile Suits Gundam Shenlong and the upgraded Gundam Altlong. The original Gundam Shenlong's fate was destroyed by OZ when Wufei was imprisoned with Duo and Heero. Yet the dust had hardly settled from the

Shenlong when Professor G (captured at the same time as Wufei) had Gundam Altlong ready for Wufei.

When Wufei got his new suit, he went on a rampage through space and destroyed any and every Mobile Suit he saw, regardless of the people's pleas, beliefs or cries. Wufei didn't care why they were fighting; if they were fighting they were wrong, and they therefore deserved to be executed on the spot.

Is Wufei a murderer or an avenging angel? The series doesn't come down on either side. It's left for you to decide. ➜

Chang Wufei

The Gundam Files

Trowa Barton

Mobile Suit: Gundam Heavyarms
Age: 15
Sex: Male
Ethnicity: Unknown
Origin: Colony LaGrange Point 3
Family: Unknown (adopted sister, Catherine Bloom)
Height: 160 cm
Weight: 44 kg
Eye Color: Green
Hair Color: Brown

The name Trowa Barton strikes fear into the hearts of those who oppose him – and it's not even the real name of the pilot who uses it. The original pilot of Gundam Heavyarms was named Trowa Barton, but when he was shot (as explained in Endless Waltz), a young mechanic who worked on the Gundam (and who had been a mercenary earlier in life) volunteered to pilot Gundam Heavyarms and fulfill Operation Meteor.

Later, an undercover Trowa joined up with a traveling carnival as a clown/knife-thrower/horseback-rider/lion-tamer. There he met Catherine Bloom, a girl who adopted him as her brother. Later in the series, Trowa lost his memory and rejoined the carnival, only to leave for the war once he is nursed back to health.

That's about all that's known about Trowa's past, and Trowa isn't exactly forthcoming with the details. Trowa's a lot like Heero – silent and deadly. Rather than explaining his actions like many of the other pilots, Trowa fights because he knows his goal.

Trowa Barton

As you might expect, Trowa and Heero develop close ties. In fact, Heero is the only person in the series to make Trowa laugh. True, Heero does so by nearly killing himself when he engages the self-destruct feature of his Gundam, but it is still evidence of their bond.

True to its name, Trowa's Heavyarms is the most heavily armed of the Gundams. Packing anywhere from 36 to 48 missiles and carrying a heavily loaded machine gun in addition to the standard Gundam machine guns, Heavyarms is meant for slugging it out in ground combat. Later in the series it's modified for space combat, but even then it's very sluggish. Fortunately, its powerful weapons heavily outweigh its clumsiness.

OZ Characters

Zechs Merquise/ Milliardo Peacecraft

Mobile Suit: Gundam Epyon
Age: 19
Sex: Male
Ethnicity: Northern European
Origin: Sanc Kingdom, Earth
Family: Relena Darlian/Peacecraft (sister)

Zechs Merquise

joined the White Fang, but only to lead them to defeat.

The soldier side of Zechs' personality craves action and will not be appeased. Zechs is always on the lookout for a good battle, regardless of which side he joins. For example, when he found Heero rebuilding Gundam Wing, he fought him just like he did before Heero self-destructed. That whole event was the result of Zechs' inability to control his urge to fight.

In the end, Zechs/Milliardo dedicated himself to reclaiming his parents' dream of peace. But because he was trained as a soldier and knew no other way to attain peace than to destroy those who opposed him, Zechs used war as his way to peace. He tried to lead the world to peace by demonstrating the horror of wars. He destroyed the lives of everyone he loved, as well as his own, because of his misguided attempt to save them. Intending to give freely of himself, he wound up destroying other people.

Treize Kushrenada

Mobile Suit: Tallgeese
Age: 24
Sex: Male
Ethnicity: Presumably German
Origin: Unknown
Family: Dorothy Catalonia (niece), Duke Dermail (brother)
Height: 181 cm
Weight: 68 kg
Eye Color: Blue
Hair Color: Brown

Height: 184 cm
Weight: 76 kg
Eye Color: Blue
Hair Color: Blonde

Zechs Merquise is a man of many masks – masks that conceal many things, but masks that also bear scars.

Born Milliardo Peacecraft, heir to the ruling family of the peace-loving Sanc Kingdom, the "Lightning Baron" was orphaned as a young boy. Young Milliardo was taken in by the ambitious Treize Kushrenada. Under Treize's influence, Milliardo developed into a dedicated and accomplished soldier. Although never shown as a part of the Gundam series, it's suggested that

Milliardo took the mask and the name Zechs Merquise when he first killed a man. Ashamed by having strayed so far from his parents' teachings of total pacifism, Zechs took to wearing a mask which he would always wear in battle.

Throughout the series, Zechs constantly changes sides. Originally Zechs fought faithfully for OZ. However, due to Lady Une's actions during a Gundam raid, Zechs was forced to defy OZ. Then Zechs fought along side and against the Gundams at the same time he battled OZ. Later Zechs disappeared, only to return as Milliardo Peacecraft, who worked to restore peace in the name of the Sanc Kingdom. Then he opposed OZ/Romefeller again, using the name and mask of Zechs Merquise. In the end, he

Treize Kushrenada is never the man you think he is. He's always something more: more complex, more intelligent, more ruthless. Never once does Treize falter in pursuit of his goals. Treize can be described as the only character in Gundam Wing who ➜

The Gundam Files

has a carefully calculated reason for everything he does. And Treize knows every move made by every other person in the Gundam Wing series.

If you look at what Treize does in a particular episode, it might not make any sense – until several episodes later when everything falls into place. A perfect example of this was when Treize resigned from the OZ leadership. At first glance it didn't seem to fit the basic ruthlessness of his character. He loses all his power, he can't affect anything, and he's basically dropped out of the story.

But his resignation had a domino effect. The Romefeller Foundation split into two parts – the Treize Faction and the Romefeller group – which began battling each other. Their battle moved into space, and the colonies seized the opportunity to launch their revolution and create White Fang. Then Turbarov was killed, the Mobile Dolls were immobilized and Romefeller grew weak and needed a new leader. Queen Relena assumed control, White Fang declared war on Earth and Treize was able to step in and supplant the feeble-minded Queen Relena, and bingo! – Treize regained control of both OZ and the Romefeller Foundation. Treize could tell how all these events would play out, so he carefully laid his plans ahead of time. He figured if he weakened the entire organization, he could tear it apart and then rebuild it even stronger.

Treize piloted many different Mobile Suits throughout the series, but it's the second-form Tallgeese which Treize used for his final combat. Treize also designed and built Epyon, which he gave to Heero Yuy. This is yet another example of how Treize manipulated the other characters, this time by forcing Heero to his limits.

Treize Kushrenada

Lady Une

Mobile Suit: n/a
Age: 19
Sex: Female
Ethnicity: Unknown
Origin: Unknown
Family: Unknown
Height: Unknown
Weight: Unknown
Eye Color: Brown
Hair Color: Brown

Every good anime has to have at least one person with a split personality. Miss Une fills that role in *Gundam Wing*. Known as either Lady Une or Colonel

Une, depending on what side of the bed she got up on that morning, the woman has some serious mood swings when it comes to dealing with the colonies.

Example?

How about the infamous Episode 10, when as Colonel Une she readied a group of nuclear-missile satellites and held the colonies hostage. This was after she told Heero and the other Gundam pilots that if they didn't surrender, she would nuke every Colony Cluster from here to Mars. Her plan failed thanks to Heero and the cunning Dr. J – but the nerve!

And yet, just a few episodes later, Colonel Une has transformed into the delightful, beautiful and peace-loving Lady Une. Sent as an ambassador to the colonies, all the gentle-natured Lady Une can think about is uniting the colonies and making sure everyone lives in peace.

Interesting, huh?

Many Gundam fans trace Miss Une's identity crisis back to when she held the colonies hostage. Treize Kushrenada called up Colonel Une and told her to "have a little more class" in the way she carried out the war. Colonel Une, desperately in love with Treize and always trying to please him, created two identities out of Treize's criticism: the ruthless Colonel Une who will stop at nothing to further OZ's military aims, and the kind Lady Une who has the "class" to deal with the ethics of war.

Just as good a pilot as others in the series, Lady Une doesn't do too much battling, but she does play a key role near the end of the series by saving Treize's life using Heero's original Gundam, the Gundam Wing. After being in a coma (from injuries sustained earlier in the series), Lady Une woke up, jumped out of bed, pulled out her IVs and discovered Treize had left for space. She follows and arrives at the scene just as the Libra's main cannon is about to be blasted to smithereens by Treize. Using Gundam Wing's speed, she risked her own life to jet into combat and save Treize.

Lucrezia Noin

Mobile Suit: Various

Age: 19

Sex: Female

Ethnicity: Mediterranean

Origin: Italy

Family: Unknown

Height: 165 cm

Weight: 49 kg

Eye Color: Dark Purple

Hair Color: Black

Lucrezia Noin is another key woman in the *Gundam Wing* saga. She's yet another character who is constantly switching sides. Originally an OZ soldier and a strong supporter of Zechs Merquise, Lucrezia eventually becomes an ally of Relena Peacecraft in the Sanc Kingdom.

She sure didn't start out that way. Intercepting Chang Wufei while on a routine attack, Lucrezia evaluated him using the instrumentation of her standard Leo suit. Bad idea. She wrote him off as "just a boy," badly underestimating him. At the same time, Wufei underestimated Lucrezia because of her gender. Their first battle ended in a draw and both headed their separate ways.

Early on, Lucrezia was so taken with Zechs Merquise that she followed him around like a little puppy dog and hung on his every word. She was always eager to please him. In fact, Lucrezia was so desperately in love with Zechs that she would even take Relena under her wing.

We never really know for sure, but Zechs probably asks her to do this because he knows Relena is his sister and he doesn't want anything to happen to her. At any rate, Lucrezia and Relena learned much from each other. Lucrezia learned how powerful ➔

Lucrezia Noin

The Gundam Files

peace really is, and Relena found out how politics really work.

The two women stayed together and helped each other. Lucrezia eventually adopted Relena's ideas and helped her rebuild the Sanc Kingdom. Even though the reborn Sanc Kingdom was still committed to total pacifism, Lucrezia insisted on protecting the kingdom from those who invaded it.

True to the unpredictability of *Gundam Wing*, Lucrezia's storyline got a dramatic plot twist in the end. Love prevailed when Lucrezia and Zechs finally met up, and when faced with whether to join Zechs or continue to fight for what she truly believes ...she crumbles. Love triumphs after all, gosh darn it.

If there were an award for "Most Provoked Character," it would have to go to Lucrezia Noin. She's certainly had to face more than her fair share of emotional upheaval.

Lucrezia Noin

Civilians

Relena Darlian/ Peacecraft

Mobile Suit: n/a
Age: 15
Sex: Female
Ethnicity: Northern European
Origin: Sanc Kingdom
Family: Milliardo Peacecraft (brother)
Height: 154 cm
Weight: 38 kg
Eye Color: Blue
Hair Color: Brown

Relena Darlian/Peacecraft is the proverbial Angel of the Battlefield. She has constantly argued for a peaceful settlement to all disputes and worked tirelessly to end the war. She is a true pacifist, and the world of Gundam Wing would be in ashes without her.

Relena first appeared as the daughter of Darlian, Earth's Peace Ambassador. When she accompanied him on a trip to Outer Space, Relena witnessed her father's assassination at the hands of Colonel Une. As he lay dying, her father revealed to Relena that she was orphaned at a young age and that she is really the heiress to the Sanc Kingdom, a now-destroyed country. It wasn't until later that she discovered that the rogue OZ pilot Zechs Merquise is really her brother, Milliardo Peacecraft.

Relena continued to learn about her past as she got mixed up with all the Gundam pilots, especially Heero Yuy. Although it isn't thoroughly explained in the series, there is a romantic connection between the young Mobile Suit ace and Relena. This is very interesting when you consider that the first time Heero met Relena, he attempted to commit suicide, and the second time he saw her, he told her to stay out of his way or he would kill her.

While Relena will never have the skills or strength to be a Gundam pilot, she can hold her own when it comes to battling the forces of evil. With the help of her butler (don't ask), Relena rebuilt the Sanc Kingdom and used the country as a place of refuge from the war.

She also founded a school for daughters of world leaders, where she meets her evil rival, Dorothy Catalinia. Different as night and day, Dorothy and Relena represent the eternal struggle between humankind's urge to conquer and dominate and its ideal of being civil and peaceful. In the end, Relena's pacifism adds much-needed philosophical balance to *Gundam Wing*.

Doctor J

Doctor J is the Gundam Scientist from the L1 Colony Cluster who designed the Gundam Wing. Easily recognizable by his robotic arm and goggles, Doctor J is probably the most frequently seen of all the Gundam Scientists.

Doctor S

Doctor S is the Gundam Scientist from the L3 Colony Cluster who is renowned for his fake nose. (Why? Don't ask.) Even though he created the Gundam Heavyarms, he had nothing to do with training Trowa Barton.

Instructor H

Hailing from the L4 Colony Cluster, Instructor H is perhaps the one and only normal-looking Gundam Scientist – as normal as a mad scientist can get, anyway. Instructor H is responsible for Gundam Sandrock and for training Quatre Winner. He's also the one who saved the Wing ZERO plans.

Master O

The final Colony Cluster, L5, provided a home to the strong, silent Master O. Master O is recognized by his extremely large stature and bald head. Master O created the sleek Gundam Shenlong and is responsible for instructing its pilot, Wufei.

Howard

Although we have no clue where he comes from, and he isn't one of the five Gundam Scientists, Howard plays a key role in the series. Not only did he help Duo fix his ship, but he also designed the Tallgeese and the Peacemillion Gundams. His Hawaiian shirt is a dead giveaway.

Professor G

Professor G is the Gundam Scientist from the L2 Colony Cluster. He has a shaggy mop of hair with a large white nose protruding out of it. An expert in stealth technology, Professor G created Gundam Deathscythe. Duo Maxwell is the former student of this sometimes-mad scientist. ■

Relena Darlian/Peacecraft

Mobile Suit Mania

Check out the stats on your favorite (or least favorite) mobile suits

GUNDAM DEATHSCYTHE IS the Gundam that almost never was. It was almost destroyed by its pilot, Duo Maxwell, before it was even sent to Earth (as seen in a flashback in *Endless Waltz*). Thank goodness the designer and creator of Gundam Deathscythe, Professor G, knew that Duo might try destroying it when he found out the real intentions of Operation Meteor (read "The Politics of Gundam Wing" on page 72 for more info) and disabled the self-destruct mechanism.

The Gundam Deathscythe is a favorite among Gundam fans, overshadowed only by its successor, Gundam Deathscythe Hell. It's easy to see why the Deathscythe is so loved. Just take a look at the way the thing looks and you'll be hooked too. And the only things greater than the design are the weapons that accompany it.

The Gundam Deathscythe's Beam Scythe is unique. Besides being the only thermo-weapon that can be used under water (as we see when Duo uses it to retrieve the sunken Gundam Wing), it's great at slicing, dicing and destroying anything in its path. The sickle-shaped, Grim Reaper-influenced Beam Scythe is a perfect match for Duo, the self-proclaimed God of Death, and the standard double machine guns, Buster Shield and radar jammers only add to the fun of it.

Gundam Deathscythe

Name: Pilot: Duo Maxwell
Registry Number: XXXG-01D
Height: 16.3 m
Weight: 7.2 tons
Material: gundanium

Only its successor, Gundam Deathscythe Hell, can match the popularity of the original Deathscythe.

Gundam Altron

Pilot: Chang Wufei
Registry Number: XXXG-01S2
Height: 16.4 m
Weight: 7.5 tons
Material: gundanium

Stealth is the name of the game for Gundam Deathscythe. Sneaking up on unsuspecting bases, opponents and Mobile Suits, it can get in and get out before anyone even realizes something (or someone) has been destroyed.

Of course, what would a Gundam be without being destroyed once or twice?

Gundam Deathscythe eventually falls into the hands of the enemies, though Duo tries unsuccessfully to destroy it. As a testament to their power, the OZ forces used Deathscythe as "target" practice for the newly made Vayeate on live satellite TV. From that point on, Deathscythe joined the ranks of the destroyed.

But don't worry; a new version of Deathscythe was soon created. You don't mess with success.

Gundam Altron

Gundam Altron is the highly destructive upgrade of the Gundam Shenlong. Call it Shenlong 2.0. When Wufei's Gundam Shenlong and Duo's Deathscythe were destroyed, the Scientists had to start on new versions of each Mobile Suit, thus Altron was formed. Expanding on the original Shenlong's greatest features while retaining the dragon-like look, the Gundam Altron is one awesome system.

Where the Shenlong only used a single Dragon's Claw, the Gundam Altron has Dragon's Claws on both arms. The Dragon's Claws are also retractable and *really* extendible. (Don't ask us how they fit nearly 100 feet of solid Gundanium in that thing for it to shoot out, but those wacky Gundam Scientists figured it out.)

The Shenlong's Beam Glaive was

Gundam Altron's Dragon Claws can extend up to 100 feet.

replaced by a much spiffier, much more deadly Double-Ended Beam Trident. Altron also carries a lot more firepower than its predecessor, thanks to twin Vulcan Guns on the side of each Dragon's Claw and Plasma Rifles attached to a tail-like extension.

One of the most common misunderstandings about Gundam Altron is that it has a ZERO system. Sorry, but there's no evidence in the series even

suggesting a ZERO System was installed. People think that Wufei goes on a rampage through space using Altron because of the ZERO System's influence on him, when it's really just Wufei venting. There isn't too much evidence suggesting a ZERO System isn't installed, either. But if the Gundam Scientists all agreed that Wing ZERO's system was too powerful and ➔

Unusually thick armor and a big, heavy shield make Sandrock tough to take down.

Gundam Sandrock

Pilot: Quatre Raberba Winner
Registry Number: XXXG-01SR
Height: 16.5 m
Weight: 7.5 tons
Material: gundanium

Vayeate

Pilot: Trowa Barton (Doll System)
Registry Number: OZ-13MSX1
Height: 16.3 m
Weight: 7.3 tons
Material: gundanium

deadly, why would they put it into other versions of their Gundams?

While you never see Gundam Altron join the destroyed list in *Gundam Wing*, there's always *Endless Waltz*. Guess you'll have to wait to find out.

Gundam Sandrock

Gundam Sandrock is modeled after Gundam Heavyarms. In other words, it goes for power, not mobility. Built by the eccentric Instructor H and piloted by the

Later in the series, like Heavy Arms, Gundam Sandrock had to be adjusted for space warfare. The transformation was successful. Quatre uses Sandrock in space as if it were in the deserts of Africa, unleashing its Energy Sickles on more than 30 Virgo II in one battle.

The *Gundam Wing* version of Gundam Sandrock is quite often passed over in favor of the more colorful, "lighter" Hajime Katoki/*Endless Waltz* version, despite the fact that the two are near equals.

data from Heero and Trowa's original flight.

When given the right pilots, these suits are surpassed only by the Wing ZERO and Epyon. Mercurius and Vayeate work as a team to bring the best defense and the most powerful offense to the battlefield, making them greater in power than any other single suit.

Mercurius uses its large Electromagnetic Force Shield (the 10 mine-looking plates you see on its back) to block any energy attack hurtled at it. Its large Crash Shield

Mercurius

Pilot: Heero Yuy
Registry Number: OZ-13MSX2
Height: 16.3 m
Weight: 7.3 tons
Material: gundanium

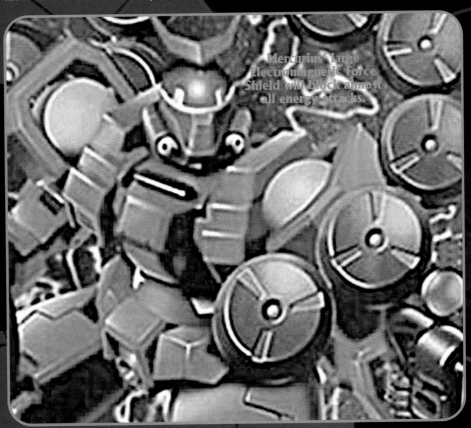

Mercurius' large Electromagnetic Force Shield will block almost all energy attacks.

peaceful Quatre, Gundam Sandrock moves like molasses on a cold day. But just like molasses, the all-terrain Sandrock is the main ingredient in some real sweet goodies.

Sandrock's main weapons are large Energy Sickles which destroy their targets on contact. Sandrock also has pistol-like weapons called Vulcans as well as standard machine guns mounted near the neck.

Sandrock features a load of armor. The Gundam has an abnormally thick Mobile Suit backed by a large shield planted on its left arm. This gives Quatre time to set up his opponent and use his offensives.

The Sandrock was originally self-detonated right before Quatre went into space. But remember: a Gundam never dies. The OZ forces took Sandrock in for study, while Quatre's allies, the Maganacs, stole it right back and restored the Mobile Suit good as new.

Vayeate/Mercurius

Vayeate and Mercurius are Mobile Suits in a class of their own, formidable by themselves but even greater when put together. The designers of the deadly duo, the five original Gundam Scientists, obviously used the age-old peanut-butter-and-jelly equation to create the team-up Mobile Suits. And you know what? It works great.

Though no pilot gets either version full-time, when we see them, Heero Yuy runs the Mercurius and Trowa Barton pilots the Vayeate. Later in the series we see Doll systems placed into the suits using the

enables it to charge opponents, blasting energy from its shield as it goes. If Mercurius' defenses fail, it's also armed with a short-range Plasma Gun for fighting off any oncoming opponents.

Vayeate is the exact opposite of the Mercurius; mobility and firepower are its hallmarks. Its large back-mounted plate is used as a Solar Conductor to supply energy to operate its large Plasma Rifle. The rifle can fire a large powerful beam or short, equally powerful, blasts of energy.

The Vayeate was blasted into uselessness by the Wing ZERO. However, its wreckage was recovered and restored alongside the Mercurius, both of which ➜

Gundam Epyon

Name: Pilot: Heero Yuy, Zechs Merquise
Registry Number: OZ-13MS
Height: 17.4 m
Weight: 8.5 tons
Material: gundanium

Epyon's ZERO system transfers information to its pilot's brain.

ran on Doll systems until The God of Death, Duo Maxwell, destroyed them both in a one-on-two battle.

Guess those Doll systems aren't nearly as effective as we thought.

Virgo/Virgo II

The Virgo is OZ's greatest Mobile Doll. Created by Turbarov, who believed that unmanned Mobile Suits could compete with the Gundams, the Virgo succeeded beyond all expectations.

The Virgo has four of the same type of Electromagnetic Force Shields given to Mercurius. A group of Virgos can create a sphere-like shield, completely protecting them from energy attack. Hiding behind their powerful shields, the Virgos use their Plasma Cannons to attack opponents.

The Virgos are invincible to most Mobile Suits, but they have one large flaw: close-range combat. Once the Virgos are within range, they are quickly destroyed.

The original Virgo was used mainly to crush resistance on Earth. Though its design was indeed revolutionary, its Doll system let it down. It turns out old-fashioned human pilots can wax a Doll any day.

The Virgo II, which looks like an entirely new Mobile Suit, has about the same type and amount of weaponry. The standard Plasma Cannon was dropped in favor of more powerful carry-on cannons. The Virgo II was used only by the White Fang and appears to be designed specifically for space combat, but this is never proven in the series.

More Mobile Suits

Virgo

Pilot: None, Mobile Doll
Height: 16.5 m
Weight: 7.4 tons
Model Number: OZ-02MD
Material: Titanium

Virgo II

Pilot: None, Mobile Doll
Height: 16.3 m
Weight: 7.9 tons
Model Number: OZ-03MD
Material: Titanium

Mobile Suit Aries

The Aries is one of OZ's Mobile Suits, named after the zodiac sign. It has very little effective armor and is meant for guerrilla warfare and quick combat.

Wing Gundam

Pilot: Heero Yuy
Registry Number: XXXG-01W
Height: 16.3 m
Weight: 7.1 tons
Material: gundanium

Wing Gundam or Gundam Wing? Whichever way you say it, this is one mean suit.

The Virgo II has a unique built-in piloting system – a mixture of the Doll System and the ZERO System – which enables it to go on manual when someone (namely Dorothy Catalinia of the White Fang) chooses to do so. By standing in a large room with a single helmet, the "pilot" can control a single Virgo II or an entire fleet. How the system works is a mystery, but it's speculated that by using the ZERO function, they can simultaneously decide what each Mobile Suit should do. It's a unique system, all right.

Since the Virgo II is mass-produced, it really can never be added to the destroyed list.

Gundam Epyon

Gundam Epyon is one of the two Mobile Suits known to have a ZERO system installed. And Epyon is one of the two most powerful Mobile Suits in the series – and undeniably unique.

Originally piloted by Heero Yuy, Epyon went from Heero to Zechs when he fought Heero in Round 1 of the Wing ZERO-vs.- Epyon battle. (In return, Zechs gives Heero the Wing ZERO.) From then on, Zechs/Milliardo is recognized as the Epyon's pilot.

In keeping with its special status, the Gundam Epyon is crammed with unique weapons. Its long whip-like Heat Rods can cut through any non-Gundam Mobile Suit like a hot knife through butter. The Heat Rods cater to the Epyon's speed and →

Mobile Suit Cancer

One of two underwater Mobile Suits, the crab-shaped Cancer, has absolutely no use on land. It's usually used for low-level combat missions, normally to retrieve underwater wreckage.

Mobile Suit Leo

The Leo is used for standard ground combat. It's sturdier than the Aries but is much more sluggish and only uses boosters as it touches down. Many weapons can be used to armor the Leo, including Beam Rifles, Plasma Cannons, shields and Dober Guns.

Mobile Suit Pisces

The other underwater Mobile Suit, the Pisces, is used more for attacking and underwater combat. Its large column of missiles makes it formidable against off-shore bases and other close-to-water forts.

Mobile Suit Taurus

This is a space-based Mobile Suit that can also be used on Earth. It comes in two versions: a black one used in space and a white one (which can be easily converted to plane mode) used on Earth. Both versions typically carry a Buster Cannon.

Gundam Shenlong

Pilot: Chang Wufei
Registry Number: XXXG-01S
Height: 16.4 m
Weight: 7.4 tons
Material: gundanium

Shenlong's Dragon Claws may be the suit's most feared weapon.

agility, making it a simple chore to fly by a Mobile Suit and turn it into dust. Alongside the Heat Rods is a Beam Saber hidden just under its handle for quick access.

The ZERO system installed in the Epyon is like the one installed in the Wing ZERO. It acts as a step between sense and thinking, automatically transferring information on the Epyon's opponent to the pilot's brain and suggesting a reaction for the pilot. The ZERO system takes virtual control of the opponent's mind, making him see what will happen next and trying to force him to react the suggested way.

The Epyon is also one of two Mobile Suits with a built-in Bird Mode. Like the old Japanese-anime Transformers, Epyon can quickly convert to a plane for even faster travel. This makes the Epyon perfect for any type of travel and terrain.

The Gundam Epyon is also interesting because Heero could master the Wing ZERO's ZERO system but not the Epyon's ZERO system. There's evidence that Treize had a hand in it when Heero tells Zechs, "You can have [the Epyon]. I don't know how Treize thinks," implying that Treize gave his own spin to the Mobile Suit.

In the end, it's assumed that Epyon joins the list of the destroyed Mobile Suits, but we can't really be sure – especially in the world of *Gundam Wing*.

Gundam Wing

Gundam Wing – we have no clue why the series was named after this particular Gundam, but it was. Gundam Wing, the creation of our favorite mad scientist, Dr. J, is a mix of the other four main Gundams (Gundam Sandrock, Gundam Heavyarms, Gundam Deathscythe and Gundam Shenlong). Piloted by the implied main character Heero Yuy, Gundam Wing is your run-of-the-mill transforming mecha (excuse me – Mobile Suit! We're in the Gundam Universe) with the ability to change into a bird-like jet and battle in its humanoid figure as well. In fact, the ability to transform into a jet gave Gundam Wing its name.

Besides its transforming ability, the Gundam Wing has some other awesome qualities. Its Buster Cannon allowed Heero to take out two Mobile Suits with a single blast. However, the Gundam Wing was really built for close combat. Heero uses his Beam Saber like a fish uses its gills, and the Buster Shield on the Gundam's left arm helps it ward off practically anything.

Gundam Wing probably has the most interesting "destroyed" history of all the Gundams. Heero first drops it into the ocean and thinks it's gone, but Duo recovers it. Then, in the infamous Episode 10, Heero officially self-destructs, destroying the Gundam Wing and himself.

but it returns a few episodes later, when Zechs has it reconstructed for Heero's use. Of course, Heero ditches it like any other piece of junk to make his flight to space. Then in the final episodes, Gundam Wing makes its final return, piloted by Lady Une, who is saving Treize.

A more appropriate name for this Mobile Suit would be *Gundam, The Cat That Came Back The Next Day*. Of course, had they given it that name, it probably wouldn't have had near the fan appeal it does now.

Gundam Wing is the standard-bearer for the series. What 14-year-old kid wouldn't want to be in the driver's seat of some 10-ton machine of pure destruction and mayhem, even for a mere 30 minutes every weekday?

Gundam Shenlong

Gundam Shenlong is the dragon-like Mobile Suit piloted by martial-arts master Chang Wufei. It's armed with a Dragon's Claw on its right arm, which can be used to grab opposing Mobile Suits and rip out anything it can. The Dragon's Claw also has a huge built-in flamethrower.

Alongside the standard machine guns, the turquoise-and-white Shenlong is armed with a Beam Glaive for close combat.

Master O, the bald Gundam scientist, built the Gundam Shenlong with a slender body build and tons of agility for martial-arts combat – and that's how Wufei uses it.

The nickname that Wufei gave the Gundam Shenlong, "Nataku," has an interesting past. In Wufei's clan, men are required to marry at 14. Wufei chose to marry the strongest woman in the clan, who was also a Mobile Suit pilot. When their colony was sent to be "disinfected" by General Septum, Wufei's wife, who called herself "Nataku," went to defend the colony – in a Tallgeese. (Meaning more than one was made.)

Wufei, seeing his wife in trouble, jumped into the Shenlong and went to help her. Unfortunately, she was killed moments after Wufei arrived. As a tribute to his wife, Wufei always calls his ➡

Gundam Heavyarms

Pilot: **Trowa Barton**
Registry Number: **XXXG-01H**
Height: **16.7 m**
Weight: **7.7 tons**
Material: **gundanium**

The aptly named Heavyarms carries six machine guns, six heat-seeking missiles and 24 short-range missiles.

Wing Gundam Zero

Pilot: Heero Yuy
(Zechs, Quatre, Trowa)
Registry Number: XXXG-00W0
Height: 16.7 m
Weight: 8.0 tons
Material: gundanium

Gundam Shenlong "Nataku."

The name "Shenlong" also has a relatively cool meaning. Some of you might recognize the name from the *Dragonball Z/GT* series. That's because "Shenlong" is Chinese for "God Dragon." Many people reverse the name – Gundam Shenlong as opposed to Shenlong Gundam. While the second is technically correct, all the U.S. versions call it "Gundam Shenlong."

The fate of the Shenlong is indeed sad. It joined the long list of MIA/destroyed Gundams.

Gundam Heavyarms

The words, "YO ADRIAN!!!" come to mind every time one looks at Gundam Heavyarms. Of course, it's possible that Heavyarms would never get roughed up in a match against anybody.

Dr. S, the Gundam Scientist who created Heavyarms, ignored everything except weapons. Gundam Heavyarms is not meant for mobility. For it to work in space, it had to be tweaked a little. Of course, when you carry one machine gun, six heat-seeking missiles, 24 short-range Scrambler missiles, four more machine guns and one Energy Machine Gun, who needs mobility? You could take out an entire colony with Heavyarms alone!

Hard as it is to believe, Gundam Heavyarms was almost destroyed when Trowa linked up with the traveling circus. Coincidentally, Trowa and crew ended up performing for a fleet of OZ soldiers. Trowa,

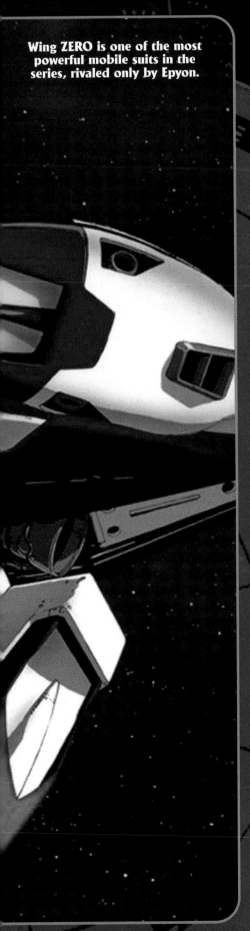

The Wing ZERO is actually the original collaboration of all five Gundam Scientists before each went their separate ways to build their own mobile suits.

envious of Heero's selfless attitude, tried to pull a self-destruction trick and take a bunch of OZ soldiers with him. Thankfully, Catherine stood up to Trowa and stopped him. (Who would have known a slender beauty like Catherine could climb up a Mobile Suit and slap the pilot in the face?)

The *Endless Waltz* version of Heavyarms looks "new" but really isn't – just different. Hajime Katoki's rendition changes Heavyarms' primary color to true blue. It's a real improvement, and it's yet another reason to watch *Endless Waltz*.

Gundam Wing ZERO

Wing ZERO. The Mobile Suit that never should have been. The Wing ZERO is actually the original collaboration of all five Gundam Scientists before each went their separate ways to build their own Gundams. The brilliance of all five is there, but the power they gave to Wing ZERO, particularly the powerful ZERO System, was just too much. Though they trashed the idea of building it, they couldn't let it go to waste, could they?

Instructor H, the tutor of Quatre Winner, hid the designs away safely inside the Winner family computers, until one day ...

In Episode 21, "Grief-Stricken Quatre," we see Quatre go through the pain of losing his father (as well as the loyalty of most of the citizens of his colony) to OZ

forces. In pain, Quatre seeks vengeance and finds the plans for the Wing ZERO. It's unclear what kind of two-day delivery they have for a Buster Cannon about as powerful as a Super Nova, but Quatre got Wing ZERO built, and quick.

Quatre takes the ZERO and destroys whatever OZ-controlled colony he can find with one shot apiece. That might seem all nice and dandy, but this isn't Quatre. Quatre is known for his peaceful attitude. What gives?

The ZERO System makes it so a pilot no longer has to think. All the pilot has to do is think of an objective and the ZERO System then builds on that objective, making sure it gets completed down to the dirtiest deed. This is what we see with Quatre.

Many people pilot the Wing ZERO throughout the series – Zechs, Quatre, Trowa, Madman #3. But Heero is the rightful pilot, one of the few who actually masters the ZERO System and can use Wing ZERO to its full extent without going insane.

Wing ZERO is one of the two most powerful Mobile Suits in the series, rivaled only by Epyon. Its weapons include a Twin Buster Cannon, which can be used separately or combined, a Beam Saber (surprise, surprise!), as well as speed that rivals the Tallgeese and a super-powerful shield.

Wing ZERO plays a prevalent role in the final battle, when Wing ZERO is the only Mobile Suit that can stop Zechs from ➜

Tallgeese

Pilot: Zechs Merquise
Registry Number: OZ-00MS
Height: 17.4 m
Weight: 8.8 tons
Material: Titanium

Tallgeese was eventually scrapped for putting too much pressure on its pilots.

dropping the Libra on Earth and successfully blowing the falling battleships into oblivion.

Of all the Mobile Suits in the series, Wing ZERO is the only one that touches every aspect of the series. Of course, not too many other piloting systems make their pilots go insane.

Tallgeese/Tallgeese II

Tallgeese was originally a prototype of the Leo suit, built by our Hawaiian-shirt-wearing friend Howard, and was trashed because of the extreme stress it placed on the pilot's body. (Check out Episode Nine, "Portrait of a Ruined Country," when Zechs takes the Mobile Suit for a spin and finds himself with broken ribs and bandages galore.)

The suit was revived by Zechs in his search for a Mobile Suit that could combat the Gundams. The Tallgeese's incredible speed makes it a match for any other Mobile Suit. The irony? The classics are always better than the new.

While the Tallgeese is thought to be original and unique, there may be copies, and it may even have been mass-produced at some point. We see this in the Episode Zero Act 7: "Wufei Manga," when Wufei's wife takes a Tallgeese into battle. Whether or not this is just a fluke, this leads us to believe there is more than one Tallgeese out there.

The Tallgeese is built for dual-purpose battling. Its speed helps it avoid close-range shots and attacks, while the Beam Saber

helps in close-range duels. Then, if needed, the Tallgeese can retreat to a safer distance and use its Dober Gun for long-range shots.

Zechs' original Tallgeese was destroyed to make way for the newest OZ Mobile Suits, Mercurius and Vayeate. However, near the end of the series, Treize Kushrenada brings a Tallgeese to the final battle. This Tallgeese is commonly referred to as Tallgeese II. The newer version doesn't seem to have any enhancements, but it may have received a boost in defense. The only real difference between the original and the newer version is the color scheme and the upper armor that Treize added, enhancing its Roman look.

Unfortunately, the Tallgeese II was destroyed during combat by a regretful Wufei, taking its newest pilot, Treize, with it. ■

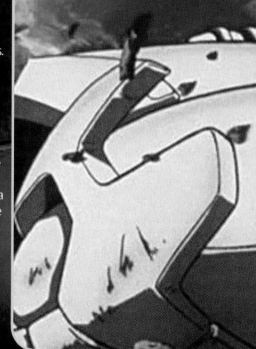

Tallgeese II

Pilot: Treize Kushrenada
Registry Number: OZ-00MS2
Height: 17.4 m
Weight: 8.8 tons
Material: Titanium

**Like the original, Tallgeese II
ultimately met its doom.**

G-Rated

The ultimate Gundam Wing episode guide

Curious whether or not you've witnessed the complete 49-episode series of Gundam Wing? Here's an episode-by-episode listing of all 49 Gundam Wing shows, with the titles roughly translated from their original Japanese. Note that while we've kept as many plot twists hidden as possible, a few tidbits are contained below. (For the fullest enjoyment, watch the entire series first!) Keep track and happy viewing!

Episode 1:
The Shining Star She Saw

The pilot episode explains much of the background for the story, the five Gundam pilots bring their mobile suits to Earth as part of "Operation Meteor," a last-ditch attempt by the space-colony scientists to free the space colonies – and all humanity – from the repressive United Earth Sphere Alliance. Five young pilots are chosen to battle the alliance using incredibly powerful mobile suits called Gundams. Each Gundam has a unique design and capabilities, and the five pilots must carry out their missions in secrecy, independent of each other. Four of the five Gundams succeed in reaching Earth in secret, but the 01 Gundam (Wing Gundam) is intercepted by ace Alliance pilot Zechs Merquise, beginning the conflict. Relena Darlian, adopted daughter of an Earth Alliance minister, sees the face of the Wing Gundam's pilot, Heero Yuy, thus starting in motion other plot twists.

Episode 2:
The Gundam Deathscythe

Heero plots against Relena and attempts to destroy the Wing Gundam, ditched into the sea. Zechs has other plans, however, with the conflict changing further when the 02 Gundam (Deathscythe) and its pilot, Duo Maxwell, join the fray.

Episode 3:
Five Gundams Confirmed

Duo's efforts free Heero from enemy hands. Zechs retreats to arm himself with the Tallgeese, a mobile suit capable of doing battle with the Gundam threat.

Episode 4:
The Victorian Nightmare

Zechs continues his battle planning, and along with his assistant, Lucrezia Noin, begins training a counterattack force at Victoria Base. But plans go awry for everyone when Chang Wufei launches a surprise attack.

Episode 5:
Relena's Secret

Relena and her father return to the Colonies, but a plot by the Earth Alliance's secret controlling society, OZ, results in the death of her father. With his dying words, Relena learns her true identity.

Episode 6:
Party Night

Relena returns to her school on Earth, thus bringing about the surprising end of her initial conflict with Heero.

Episode 7:
Scenario for Bloodshed

The plotting of Treize Khushrenada, OZ's commander, snares the Gundams and their pilots, as OZ seizes control of Earth and begins a political conquest of the space colonies.

Episode 8:
The Trieze Assassination

Treize's plotting is uncovered, with the result that OZ and the Gundams are now direct foes. Plans are made to assassinate Trieze for his duplicity.

Episode 9:
Portrait of a Ruined Country

Zechs receives his completed Tallgeese, but the new suit causes difficulties for the enigmatic Zechs, whose own motivations are slowly being revealed to the show's viewers.

Episode 10:
Heero Distracted by Defeat

The continued plotting of Lady Une (another OZ bigwig) results in further difficulties for the Gundam forces, particularly Heero.

Episode 11:
The Whereabouts of Happiness

The conflict continues between Relena and her mortal enemy, OZ's Lady Une.

Episode 12:
Bewildered Warriors

The desperate Gundam pilots, confused and in retreat, begin to hatch new plans.

Episode 13:
Catherine's Tears

Trowa begins a desperate battle as Lady Une and her OZ forces continue sweeping away the opposition.

Episode 14:
The Order to Destroy 01

Relena is called before the officers of the Romefeller Foundation. Zechs, operating independently of his superiors, attempts to bring Heero's battered and abandoned Wing Gundam back to life.

Episode 15:
To the Battleground ... Antarctica

Zechs' lieutenant, Lucrezia Noin, succeeds in bringing Heero and Trowa to Zechs' secret base at the South Pole, where a showdown awaits.

Episode 16:
The Sorrowful Battle

Zechs and Heero do battle, with Heero piloting the restored Wing Gundam suit. However, the battle is disrupted when a large Alliance force reaches the scene.

Episode 17:
Betrayed by Home Faraway

OZ's political plans continue their march as Lady Une, under Treize's orders, heads to the colonies to work for peace and strengthen their control. Public sentiment turns further against the Gundams and their pilots' violent methods.

Episode 18:
Tallgeese Destroyed

Now in control of the colonies, OZ (through Lady Une), captures the scientists who developed the Gundam suits, forcing them to begin work on an even more lethal suit design. The

captured Heero and Duo (who has infiltrated OZ as a test pilot) begin tests on the new suit design when Zechs, using a new identity, arrives.

Episode 19:
Assault on Baruji

Duo and Wufei do battle with OZ forces and are captured – but there are other plans afoot.

Episode 20:
The Lunar Base Infiltration

The scientists who have been forced by OZ to work on the new suit design are nearing the end of their task; the new suit is almost complete. Heero tries to disrupt OZ's plans for the new suits.

Episode 21:
Grief-Stricken Quatre

Quatre, who has returned to his father's factory asteroid, watches in horror as the other colonists shun his father's leadership and place OZ in control. Quatre's father breaks the asteroid free of the surrounding colonies, attempting to prevent OZ's evil plans for it, and the colonists respond by blasting the asteroid to pieces. The anguished Quatre seeks vengeance, and reveals plans for "The Zero System," an advancement to the Gundam design that had been abandoned due to the danger it could bring to the suit's pilot. The Zero System, which interacts directly with the pilot's brain and nervous system, adds to each suit's capabilities at a terrible price – it can drive some mobile-suit pilots insane. Insane or not, the Zero System always brings lasting changes to a pilot's personality.

Episode 22:
The Fight for Independence

Quatre seeks vengeance for his father's death by attacking the OZ-controlled forces, and Lady Une plans an appropriate response to the rampage.

Episode 23:
Duo, the Great Destroyer Once Again

Duo's plot to infiltrate the moon base and halt the production of new mobile suits being assembled there takes an unsuspected turn.

Episode 24:
The Gundam They Called Zero

Trowa and the forced-to-comply Heero do battle with the crazed Quatre.

Episode 25:
Quatre vs. Heero

Quatre's Zero System suit is indeed vastly increased in power. In the course of the battle between the Gundam pilots, Trowa faces an impossible choice. Meanwhile, OZ's machinations take a turn for the strange: Trieze splits from the Romefeller Foundation and resigns as OZ's commander, causing a split in control of the OZ forces.

Episode 26:
The Eternal Flame of the Shining Star

With the Romefeller Foundation now in control of the colonies, "Operation Nova" begins, with waves of mobile dolls being sent to Earth to crush opposition. Meanwhile OZ pilot Zechs Merquise leads the defense.

Episode 27:
The Locust of Victory and Defeat

The split between OZ factions has placed Duo, Wufei and the scientists who developed the suits in mortal peril.

Episode 28:
Passing Destinies

Trieze is captured by the Romefeller Foundation forces and is held at their headquarters, where he is forced to reevaluate his actions and begin developing a new Gundam suit.

Episode 29:
The Heroine of the Battlefield

Relena, restored to her birthright, assumes the leadership of the resurrected and peace-loving Sanc Kingdom. But the Kingdom's existence is in opposition to Romefeller Foundation plans.

Episode 30:
The Reunion with Relena

Having returned to Earth, Heero and Quatre find their way to Relena's Sanc Kingdom.

Episode 31:
The Glass Sanc Kingdom

Heero and Quatre begin a new life within the Sanc Kingdom, but when the Romefeller Foundation forces attack, the two young pilots are the new kingdom's only hope.

Episode 32:
The Great Destroyer Meets Zero

Knowledge of the Zero System's capabilities means much to those who seek power. Duo is forced to do battle with one of these seekers.

Episode 33:
The Lonely Battlefield

The Romefeller Foundation begins its attack on Trieze's Luxenbourg headquarters. They also set a trap to ensnare Zechs Merquise.

Episode 34:
And Its Name is Epyon

Heero reaches Luxenbourg just in time to see the collapse of Trieze's forces, but receives a "gift" from Trieze – the new Gundam Epyon suit, also equipped with the Zero System.

Episode 35:
The Return of Wufei

Wufei resumes his duties as a Gundam pilot, then sees his clan's code of honor in action, with tragic results. Zechs contacts Wufei to try to enlist the Gundam pilots in his cause.

Episode 36:
The Collapse of the Sanc Kingdom

The Romefeller Foundation launches its final assault on Relena's Sanc Kingdom. Relena surrenders the kingdom rather then seeing it obliterated.

Episode 37:
Zero vs. Epyon

Zechs and Heero fight an epic battle in their Zero System-augmented mobile suits. Meanwhile, the captured Relena is brought to Romefeller Foundation headquarters.

Episode 38:
Relena Becomes Queen

Now in control of the Earth, Relena accepts a surprising offer from the Romefeller Foundation to legitimize their government by serving as a respected figurehead. In return, she is able to accomplish real good among the Foundation's members by convincing them to use their new-found control for the good of mankind. However, the Foundation's newly peaceful course will soon be tested – an armed resistance group called White Fang begins seizing control of the space colonies, seeking to win the colonies' independence from Earth.

Episode 39:
Trowa Returns to the Battlefield

White Fang's leader turns out to be one of the original Operation Meteor masterminds, an enigmatic man named Quinze. Under his leadership, White Fang works to seize the Romefeller Foundation's ultimate weapon, a space fortress named Libra.

Episode 40:
A New Leader

Like the Foundation, White Fang needs a charismatic leader for its government. Enter Zechs Merquise, the Romefeller Foundation's sworn enemy, who quickly denies its authority and declares the space colonies independent from Earth's control. Zechs quickly steers White Fang in directions not intended by Quinze.

Episode 41:
Crossfire at Baruji

Baruji is the key to space supremacy, so naturally a battle ensues. The White Fang threat strikes the peaceful government of Relena at a horrible time, and a panicked faction still under Trieze's control overthrows Relena, who flees into space.

Episode 42:
Battleship Libra

Tensions build in anticipation of the final battles. Wufei's experiences with his own suit's Zero System lead him to a harsh conclusion — both Trieze and Zechs must be eliminated for the sake of humanity. And true to form, Zechs orders Libra into a position more suited for attacking the Earth.

Episode 43:
Target: Earth

Events reunite the five Gundam pilots at the space fortress Peacemillion, where they plan their parts in the upcoming conflict. Meanwhile, Zechs begins his assault on the Earth forces using the Libra's powerful weaponry.

Episode 44:
Go Forth, Gundam Team

The pilots begin their assault on Zechs and the White Fang forces, only to face an unexpected surprise: Zechs has adapted the capabilities of the Zero System to create a legion of mobile dolls, pilotless versions of mobile suits that can be operated *en masse* by remote control.

Episode 45:
Signs of the Final Battle

The Gundam pilots learn the key to defeating the mobile dolls in a daring rescue of key data from the Libra's control systems. Duo defeats two mobile dolls in the process, but the prospect of huge numbers of the suits attacking anywhere remains an overpowering threat.

Episode 46:
Milliardo's Decision

Zechs' White Fang forces quickly demonstrate their superiority, and Trieze tries to avert an all-out disaster for Earth by challenging Zechs, once driven only by honor, to a one-on-one duel. But Zechs is no longer the same person, and he responds with a blast from the Libra's main gun. Earth's cause is almost hopeless, and Trieze orders his forces into a surely suicidal attack on the Libra.

Episode 47:
Collision In Space

As the forces of Zechs and Trieze do battle, the Gundam pilots see the opportunity to change the course of the way. They crash their space fortress, the Peacemillion, into the Libra. The crash eliminates the threat of the Libra's main gun.

Episode 48:
Take Off Into Confusion

Zechs realizes that the Libra might be weaponless, except that the Libra itself might be used as a weapon. Zechs thereby orders the Libra, still entangled with the Peacemillion, into a crash descent onto the Earth itself. Heero challenges Zechs to a final duel (they've met many times previously) in a last-ditch attempt to gain control over the Libra. Meanwhile, Wufei still has a score to settle with Trieze.

Episode 49:
Final Victors

Since the two space fortresses, the Libra and the Peacemillion, are still entangled, the scientists who originally hatched Operation Meteor — note the irony — attempt to stop the descent of Libra by counteracting its descent with the Peacemillion's own engines. The attempt is only partially successful. The Peacemillion explodes from the strain, with the scientists and Quinze onboard, but a huge chunk of the Libra remains intact, descending toward a fateful impact with the Earth. And only Heero and Zechs, still waging their battle, have the capabilities to do anything about it. (We'll leave the last little bit of the story untold. To find out the surprising outcome, you'll just have to wait and watch!) ∎

Gundam

Deja-vu TCG packs a minor wallop

In the early 1990s, Richard Garfield revolutionized the way people think about and play games by taking the actions and themes of role-playing games and putting them on playing cards. While hundreds of ways had been devised to play with a "normal" poker deck and

scores of self-contained card games have been released, no one had ever seen anything like the trading card game.

The combination of baseball-card-style collectibility with true game playability has proved irresistible and has spawned countless imitators.

The TCG has become a mainstay of the gaming business and a key licensed product for any remotely popular property. It's no wonder that manufacturers of everything from Dragonball Z to Sailor Moon, and even titles that are as relatively

War

By Edward T. Hrzic III

obscure as Cardcaptors, rush to produce a TCG as soon as the action figure and plush licenses are squared away.

So who would expect Gundam Wing to be any different? Upper Deck has already announced it will soon be bringing Gundam Wing trading cards and TCGs to North America. In Japan, Gundam War is already a well-established trading card game, even though it may not be the most complex and challenging TCG you'll ever play.

Since the day that Gundam Wing made its atom-bomb impact on the Cartoon Network, North American fans have been clamoring for a Gundam game. So how does Gundam War stack up against other TCGs on the market? →

Gundam War

Unfortunately, not very well. Ever since Wizards of the Coast patented several mechanics of the Magic: The Gathering TCG (such as "tapping" – turning a card 90 degrees to indicate that an effect has been used), companies have been struggling to create TCGs that are more creative. The designers of Gundam War probably struggled as much as anyone, but the TCG they created fell short in several areas.

First of all, let's get one thing straight: This is not the Gundam Wing TCG; this is a game based on all the Gundam storylines, many of which haven't been widely seen in North America. Gundam Wing is just a small part of the Gundam universe. If you're looking for cards from the Gundam Wing show, pick up the fourth expansion of booster packs and starter decks (the ones with Heero Yuy) on the cover. If you want more Wing and less Gundam, wait for the Upper Deck products later this year.

There are five different card types in

Gundam War: Unit Cards (Mobile Suits and aircraft, used to attack your opponent), Pilot Cards (which "attach" to the Unit Cards to give them bonuses), Operation Cards (played during your turn, they stay in play to give your cards added bonuses), Command Cards (one-shot cards that produce an effect and are then discarded but can be played during an opponent's turn), and Generation Cards (which bring other cards into play).

There are also six different "factions" in the game: Earth Federation, Principality of Zeon, Titans, Neo Zeon, Turn A and Wing.

This publication is not sponsored, endorsed, or otherwise affiliated with any of the companies or the products featured in this magazine. This is not an official publication.

Each has its own Generation cards. You start your turn by drawing a card. Then once a turn you can play a Generation card. After that you can "roll" (by physically turning them 90 degrees) your Generation cards to bring Unit, Pilot, Operation and Command cards into play. However, you must roll enough Generation cards of the particular faction in order to play the card. You must also have a certain number of Generation cards in play and discard some cards from your deck.

If your Unit Cards have been in play for at least a turn, you can attack your opponent with them. Your opponent can use his Unit Cards to "intercept" your attack at this point. After intercepting, any excess offensive power your units have is dealt as damage to your opponent's deck. For each point of damage, your opponent discards one card from his or her deck.

When a player's deck has been reduced to nothing, the remaining player wins. Sound familiar? The game plays like a combination of Magic: The Gathering and Battletech, which was also designed by WotC's Richard Garfield.

Gundam War rates an "average" on the gaming scale. You've already played games like it before; at best it delivers a few new spins on one of the oldest existing TCG engines.

Currently, Gundam War has four expansions and several "Dramatic" (theme) decks. The decks are nice to have for Gundam collectors. But for serious game players, they're by no means essential. ■

High Drama Gaming

Gundam Side Story 0079 delivers a real winner to fans of anime and video games

By Greg Wilcox

Platform: Sega Dreamcast
Title: Gundam Side Story 0079
Developer/ Publisher: Bandai
Rating: T (Teen)

Despite the 20 years of success the Gundam anime has enjoyed in Japan, along with the dozens of Gundam video games that have appeared over the past decade, it's only now that U.S. fans get to play a translated version of one of those games. Fortunately it's a real winner.

Gundam Side Story 0079 for the Sega Dreamcast is a fast-paced, one-player, strategic action game, presented from a first person cockpit viewpoint. Longtime fans who have waited for the opportunity to blast Zaku Mobile Suits while piloting the famous RX-78 may be a little disappointed at the exclusion of

Gundam Side Story 0079 features nine missions of varying difficulty.

their favorite Gundams, but the game's storyline is so well-done that they really shouldn't complain. Besides, this game

shows that it takes the efforts of many to win a war, not just a powerful mech with a skilled pilot.

The amazing CGA (computer generated animation) introduction spells out the basic storyline: In UC (Universal Century) 0079, Zeon forces drop a deserted space colony on Earth in order to destroy the main Earth Federation Army base. The drop fails, in that the original target is missed, but the largest piece of the colony sends Sydney, Australia literally down under, killing many and turning the city into a huge gulf. Soon after, Zeon forces manage to overrun two-thirds of the Earth in order to secure resources for a full-scale war.

An offensive begins eleven months later, and thanks to the efforts of some skilled young pilots in experimental mobile suits (like the more familiar RX-78), the Zeon are being driven back. Shortly afterward, Australia begins its own counterattack against the enemy. This is where the game begins, and your skills are needed.

You play the game as Master Pierce Rayner (Fang 1), a former fighter pilot who now leads the White Dingo Mobile Suit squad. On your side are two other Mobile Suit pilots, Leung (Fang 2) and Mike (Fang 3), as well as Anita (Oasis), who drives a recon hover truck. Together, your mission is to support the main EFA forces as they sweep the planet clear of the Zeon army. You're basically a commando strike force, so don't worry about using what seems like excessive force – it's the Zeon who dropped a space colony on your country, remember?

The game has nine missions of varying difficulty, and there's no set way to play them, as the story changes a bit depending on whether or not you can accomplish each goal in every mission. Success in the game depends not only on your being able to take down the enemy as quickly as possible (without taking too much damage yourself), but also on your ability to give correct orders to your support team. This makes the action a bit

frantic at times, but keeping a cool head is the sign of a great leader.

The game's lightning-fast pace from start to finish makes it one heckuva rush to play. You get your mission briefing, load out your MS (mobile suit) units and hit the battlefield. No anime sequences from the Gundam series are included, and the cut scenes are all handled by the in-game engine or by short CG briefings

and updates. This means you don't find out much about the characters other than some superficial stuff. But again, this is only a side story to a much bigger conflict. It was actually quite refreshing not to have to sit through a 15-minute, angst-ridden rant given by a guy with spiky hair worrying about his battle performance.

At first, the inability to tinker with the button configuration was awkward – this

The game's lightning-fast pace keeps you glued to the screen from start to finish.

Sniper Scope mode allows you to adjust your viewpoint with the analog stick.

usually ends up being a crippling experience for newer players – but the controller layout is well-thought-out, especially since the game uses all the buttons on the Dreamcast controller. The D-pad moves your MS, double tapping it gives you a Vernier boost in one of three directions and double-tapping down twice puts you into a crouch. The analog stick is used to look around the battlefield, and it works perfectly. "X" is the weapon select, "A" is the fire button, "Y" activates the Sniper Scope (more on this in a bit) and "B" is the very helpful Lock-On button. The Left trigger can be used to either jump or hover, and the Right trigger is Guard (and acts as a sidestep when you hold Left or Right on the D-Pad). Finally, Start pauses the action and sends you to the BIC (Battle

The game doesn't include a training mode. You're tossed in the mix immediately, so you either get good in a hurry or die.

Intergration Control) System screen, where you can issue commands to your squad. While in Sniper Scope mode, you can adjust your viewpoint with the analog stick. The L and R triggers are the zoom keys in this mode, while "X," "A" and "B" have the same functions as normal. You absolutely need to get good at using your sniper skills – those easy-to-take-down

Zaku units are soon replaced by much tougher Dom and Gouf mechs, and a few boss-sized surprises also await the unprepared ...so be prepared!

Since you're supposed to be an ace Gundam jockey, there's no training mode included in the game. You'll get tossed right into the mix, and you have to get good quick!

The first two missions are great practice, so play them over a few times so you can get used to piloting your MS and keeping it off the scrap pile. There are no power-ups or extra weapons lying around in crates or popping up out of destroyed enemies or real estate, so the game plays a lot more like a simulation than an action game. By the way, you're riding the mass-produced RGM-79 or GRC-80 models, not as strong as the RX-78, but more than a match for those Zakus you'll be facing.

Later in the game, you'll have access to the RGM-79SP, a nice Sniper model MS. One mission's alternate path gives you a prototype model RX-77D to use. Should you keep it from getting blown up, finishing the game opens up some

B.I.C SYSTEM — BATTLE INTEGRATION CONTROL SYSTEM

◄ PLEASE SELECT MACHINE ►

RGM-79   NEXT ►

GARAGE : MS SELECT

Main Menu

Exit

FANG1

SHORT RANGE WEAPON
BEAM-SABER

SUB WEAPON
60mm VULCAN

SPECIAL WEAPON
HAND GRENADE

MOBILE SUIT SKILL
ARMOR
POWER
VERNIER
SPEED
SEARCH

For the most part, this is one gorgeous-looking game. Bandai went all out in making sure that all the assorted mechs and ships were exceptionally well rendered, and outside of the anime, they've never looked better. The in-game engine is also used for the movies that are sprinkled throughout the missions. The environments are also nicely detailed and destructible to some extent (buildings yes, mountains no), although a bit foggy.

Early in the game, someone says the fog is there because of all the radiation particles – another nice touch. Some of the ground textures are a bit bland, and surprisingly, the huge mechs don't kick up huge clouds of dust or leave footprints. But you won't notice this or care too much as you take out that pesky Dom

that's been trying to blow your head off.

The opening computer-generated screen is absolutely amazing; it has the look and feel of old war footage without a shot being fired.

The mechas all look great, but the people are animated a bit stiffly and look more like the cast of *Thunderbirds Are Go!*, Bandai apparently went out of the way to avoid the spiky hair, big-eyed look. The music and sound effects are really nice as well, especially if you have a good sound setup. And the voice acting is great, except for that tank driver from hell at the beginning of one of the missions.

Rayner has no lines at all – he's supposed to be you, but this comes off as odd. You constantly have people talking to you, and you can't respond. It would've been nice to have the option to respond from time to time. But these are all minor issues; the good easily outweighs the bad.

In the end, Gundam Side Story 0079 is an excellent introduction to the series' long history and a worthy purchase for fans of the Gundam team. Hopefully, Bandai will continue to bring us more and better additions to this series in the near future.

additional weapons to use for the next time you play through it.

You can finish the game rather quickly, if you know what to do, but it's worth replaying to try to get all the possible alternate paths and cinemas. It's also cool to see if you can complete certain missions with different mech configurations other than the Bob Rock approved load-outs.

The missions range from the usual search and destroy to defending a downed cargo carrier to destroying a huge laser cannon and the deadly hovering craft that shows up as just you think the mission is ending. Although you can save before or after completing them, there's no rest at all between missions. This gives the game an extra sense of energy and provides a nice running joke; every few missions someone fills you in on the progress of the Gundam RX-78's battle against the Zeon, and of course, they all think it's some sort of hoax! The way Bandai re-did some familiar scenes from the television program, using the same kind of great computer generated images as in the opening sequence, is a definite plus.

The diverse missions range from defending a downed cargo carrier to destroying a huge laser cannon.

Side Story Strategy Session

To become a master of Gundam Side Story 0079, it's important to conquer the basics first. Learn the moves by simple repetition – the controls will be confusing if you've never played a game like this.

Begin by taking the time during Missions 1 and 2 to get familiar with the basics of strafing, sniping and using your beam sword and grenades. Command Fangs 2 and 3 to go after the Zaku, while you take out the stationary targets. Don't panic if you're being bombarded by the enemy – just call for backup. Following are some more basic survival tips.

Keep Moving

The Zaku love sitting ducks, so don't be a dead duck! Always try to be in motion, or if you have to stop moving, make sure you're well hidden. Don't wade right into the path of the enemy's guns, learn to move lateral to the enemy's position without leaving the battle area. And always make good use of the Guard command; your guys will take care of you to some extent, if you let them.

Use Your Allies

First off, use Anita – she's not there just to look good. Oasis is another important asset. She can save you from some needless and deadly wandering. Have her perform a Special Search as soon as a mission starts, and also have Fangs 2 or 3 Search if the enemy isn't showing up on the map right

away. Just be prepared to fight when you spot them.

Take Your Time But Hurry Up

The missions aren't really timed, so you can explore at will. Just be aware that some events during them are time based, and you can miss out on a few things if you're not in the right place at the right time (like a new Mobile Suit to use, hint, hint ...)

Play Dirty

Two on one is good, three on one is better. Use yourself as bait and lure the enemy into the range of Fangs 2 and 3. Attack an enemy from behind as he's fighting another unit. If it's close to the end of a mission, and you see that one of the other pilots is about to lose his mech as he's fighting an enemy, lob a few grenades toward them. Your guy will eject safely, and you'll take out the enemy as well! Yes, you can shoot each other as well, so think when you plan your strategy.

Save, Save, Save

Remember to save your game before and after each mission, unless you want to re-try it if you think you missed something. There are a few different branching points, even though the main story is unchanged. You can destroy the train in mission 2, which means you don't really have to shoot down the giant Gaw in the next mission, for example.

Mission Tips

Rather than going into detail about every aspect of every mission, we'll offer a few hints on some of the harder areas in the game. Everyone will have a different battle strategy, which is the cool thing about the game. But a few of the stages can get maddening in a hurry.

Mission 2

Yes, you can destroy Visch Donahue early on (he'll be back, though...). Here's one way: Have Fangs 2 and 3 engage the enemy while you go around the right side of the map, taking out the enemy turrets and trucks and conserving your health. When you get to the train tracks, blow up the train as it approaches and don't attack Visch Donahue at all – yet.

After the cutscene, you'll have two choices: You can let him and his mechs leave the battle area, or you can wait until the two mechs near Visch begin to jet away and then open fire on them. Pause after opening fire and have Fangs 2 and 3 attack

Visch while you constantly ram him and try to get in a slice or two before he gets up. He's going to jump around a lot, and he'll try to use his whip to grab you, so do some jumping yourself (while locked on, of course). Put some distance between the two of you and have the other two Fangs close in and attack. Visch will try taking them out (hopefully), and you can hit him with a few grenades, if you're good enough. It'll take about 5 to 10 minutes to destroy him. But the cutscene afterward of Visch escaping in a truck, talking about how good you are, is worth it. It took me about 17 tries, but it can be done!

Mission 3

Head for the high ground and have Fangs 2 and 3 go after the enemy one mech at a time. (Ignore the Magella.) The Gaw moves really slow, but it drops some more Zaku onto the battlefield, which can be a pain if your guys are hurting. Aim carefully and take out the Gaw's engines quickly. You should be able to get two before it passes overhead and you have to whip out that shield (it starts dropping bombs on you!), and you can hit the other two engines after it passes you. Just stay calm.

Mission 4

Make your way over to the airstrip from the start so that you'll be able to keep an eye on the cargo truck, and protect it from getting destroyed. The powerful RX-77D is inside!

Mission 5

If you happen to miss the enemy helicopters, after the mission you're told that they were shot down by other forces in the area, so don't worry about it too much. You can dive behind the sub and sink it from underwater. Just be prepared for a tough fight afterward, because new, powerful enemy MS units show up. Use buildings for cover and jump a lot!

Mission 6

Those Doms are tough, but the giant tank that shows up is even more annoying. Try to take out the two mechs that appear, then go after the tank using long-range attacks. After it's toasted, two more Doms show up. So hopefully you've saved your strength. If you're having trouble or are in bad shape, try to lure the last one into the huge crater and deal with it by sending in one of your guys as an armed decoy as you snipe or toss a grenade or three at it.

Mission 7

Not too tough, as long as you don't fire on the nuclear reactor or get caught in the center of the map. Just keep the enemy busy (throw them a few Fangs to chew), and take them out one at a time.

Mission 8

You'll want to take your time here, because there's a big surprise near the end of the mission. Use the Fangs to go after the enemy while you boost up the mountains, taking out the guns. Dodge like mad to avoid the laser cannon fire, which steals a lot of your energy with a hit. After you deal with the last turret there's a cutscene, and you have to fight that big flying thing! Hopefully your MS is in good shape and you have at least one of your other team members to help you. Keep your distance, use the lock-on and dodge like crazy when you see that electric beam charging.

Mission 9

Visch is baaaaack. And he's got a shiny new MS-14G, which comes complete with a double-beam sword! Having had almost no success in going at it hand to hand, I have to recommend getting your guys far away and trying a headshot or two. Move Oasis well away from the action; things will soon get pretty busy. Use the Guard command if Donahue comes straight at you. After he's taken care of, have the Fangs work on the giant tank as you head for the turrets and take them out. You'll get air support to help you defeat that monster.

Again, everyone will play the game a bit differently, so what works for me may not be your cup of tea. Experiment, practice, and most of all, enjoy the game!

– Jesse LaBrocca

THE BATTLE MASTER

Gundam Wing: The Battle Master

In The Battle Master, players can assume the roles of their favorite characters from Gundam Wing.

When Bandai announced the forthcoming release of Gundam Wing: The Battle Master for PlayStation, many assumed it would be an action/strategy game along the same lines as Gundam Side Story 0079 for Dreamcast, which put players in the cockpit of a 3-D Gundam. Instead, it's a 2-D fighting game, comparable to Capcom's Street Fighter or Marvel Super Heroes series.

In Gundam Wing: The Battle Master, players can engage in combat and take on the roles of their favorite characters from the hit television series *Gundam Wing*. Word has it the Japanese version of the two-player game starred characters from a different Gundam TV series. However, Bandai, hoping to capitalize on the popularity of *Gundam Wing*, gave the game a visual facelift, which is part of the reason it's taken so long for the game to arrive in the States.

At any rate, players will be able to choose from five main characters, each with its own signature moves. Utilizing a unique "motion parts system," the game captures the mechanized sound and nature of Gundam Mobile suits. In other words, don't expect them to jump around with quite the same speed and agility as Street Fighter's Ryu or Guile.

The game is slated for a February 2001 release and will retail for $39.99.

Gundam on the PlayStation 2

Perhaps of greater interest to Gundam fans, Bandai also has an untitled Mobile Suit game in the works for Sony's PlayStation 2, which the company says will take the Gundam saga to new heights.

As Mobile Suits and battlefield scenes are rendered with the quality of computer-generated movies, players will be able to give tactical instructions to their units, including Gun Cannons, Gun Tanks and G Armors (à la Gundam Side Story 0079). Aside from the near photo-realistic graphics, what will set the game apart from Side Story is the

PlayStation 2's capability to handle far more computer-controlled opponents, making for more and smarter enemies.

The tide of the conflict hinges on the instructions a player gives his allied Mobile Suits as they go to battle. What's more, crews have their own learning curves, as they become more and more seasoned, allowing for highly strategic battles.

No matter which style of game you prefer, Y2K1 is going to be a great year for fans of Gundam video games.

– Gary Mollohan

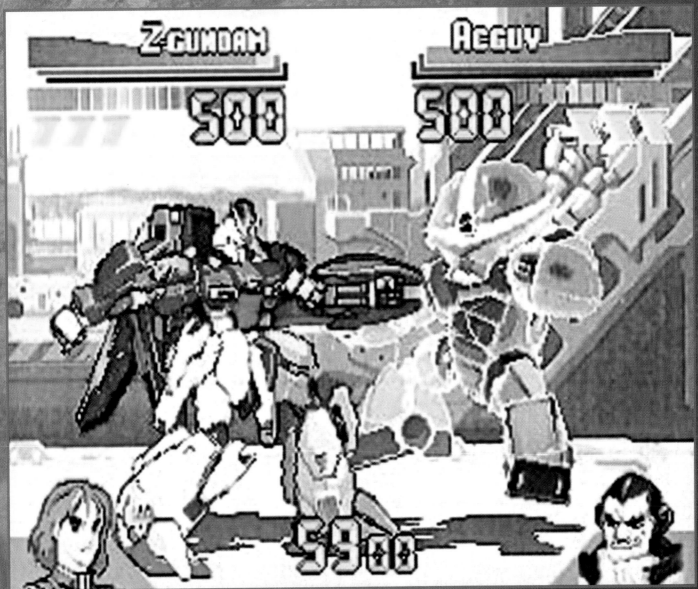

Invasion of the Plastic Warriors

Gundam modeling has diversity and flair as rich as Gundam itself

By C.T. (Core) Chin

In the U.S., modeling is sort of quaint, a sideline for enthusiasts only. But in East Asia, modeling is a huge mainstream undertaking.

Gunpla (from "Gundam plastic modeling" – it's so big in Japan they coined a word for it) started 20 years ago and seems to be getting bigger every year. Now the plastic warriors are crossing the ocean and making a bridgehead on American soil.

When the Cartoon Network broadcast commercials for Gundam Wing kits back in March, you could almost feel the whoosh as tens of thousands of fans drew in a collective gasp and ran out to buy the product. Within days, the kits were sold out in most stores. And then it got ugly: on eBay, prices went as high as 10 times the original prices.

That's all just a panic reaction. Bandai America didn't expect the models to be a hit and didn't order enough kits for the U.S. market. But a few million fans hysterical with Gunpla withdrawal is nothing new to Bandai Japan. It just takes a few months for new stocks to be manufactured and moved through the distribution network. If you're hurting for a Wing kit, just be patient; everyone will get one. In the meantime, take a look at the other Gundam model kits and maybe you'll find one or two to your liking.

In 1980, as Mobile Suit Gundam started a revolution in Japanese robot shows, Gundam models were quietly changing the face of the toy market. Inexpensive, personalized plastic kits almost single-handedly unseated Chogokin ("super alloy") toys as king of the robot hill.

Now, almost 20 years after the first Gundam kit, more than 700 different kits (including 260 superdeformed kits) have been released, and more than 350 million kits have been sold worldwide. The amazing thing is a large number of these kits are still being manufactured and are available at the original price. Demand is being renewed by kids who fall in love with the cartoons and the toys their parents loved when they were kids.

Tools of the Trade

The beauty of Gundam modeling is that most of the kits from the '90s onward are suitable for both newbies and experts. I'll list some tools and skills you need to start enjoying Gunpla. I consider Gunpla a little like martial arts: Not everyone can be a black belt, but there's no shame being a red or a white. The most important thing is participation!

White Belt

Absolutely no training is required. All you need is a cutter for removing the parts

DeathScythe Model Kit

from the runner. A pair of scissors or toenail clippers can do the job in a pinch, but spending a few dollars at Radio Shack for a pair of small wire clippers is much better. (Some modelers insist on buying clippers designed for plastic models; they're nice if you can spare the cash.)

Now pull out the instruction sheet and take a good look at it. Unless you got the domestically distributed Gundam Wing kits, you're most likely looking at an all-Japanese instruction sheet.

Don't worry: The instructions are well illustrated. Just be patient and make sure you understand each step as you cut the parts from the runners and assemble them. Apply the stickers where the instructions say. And that's it! Kids as young as 4 years old can do this. (I know because a Gundam built by a 4-year-old recently was pictured in *Hobby Japan* magazine!)

Yellow Belt

A lot of people will probably be comfortable jumping to yellow belt right away. It's still pretty easy, but it requires tools that may be dangerous around little kids. On top of the clippers, you need a sharp knife, some sandpaper or a small nail file and a permanent marker with a fine tip.

The knife can be a stationary cutter or a hobby knife. I use a surgical scalpel because it's the sharpest thing I can find, but the blade gets dull pretty quickly. A nail file can work quite well, but if you get two or three sheets of sandpaper in 400, 600 and 800 grades, the results will be better.

The permanent marker can be found in stationery stores, but an art supply store will have a better selection. Get the finest tip you can find; several companies make 0.05 mm pens, which are great.

In some hobby shops that specialize in Japanese imports, you may be able to find "Gundam Markers." Two types exist: one for painting large surfaces; the other for panel lines. Get the one for panel lines, as you may want to get all three colors (black, gray and brown).

So what does a yellow belt do? Before you assemble the parts, use the knife and sandpaper to smooth out the rough marks left from cutting them off the runners. Use the knife to cut off most of the excess plastic. Now use the 400 sandpaper to smooth it out a bit, then switch to 600 and finish it off with the 800-grade

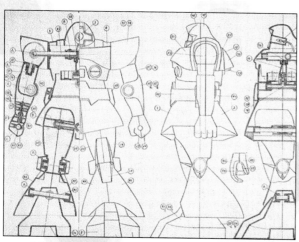

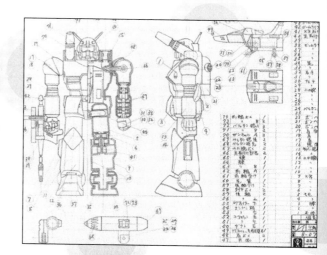

**Left:
Rick Dom
model design
from 1980**

**Right:
Guncannon
model design
from 1980**

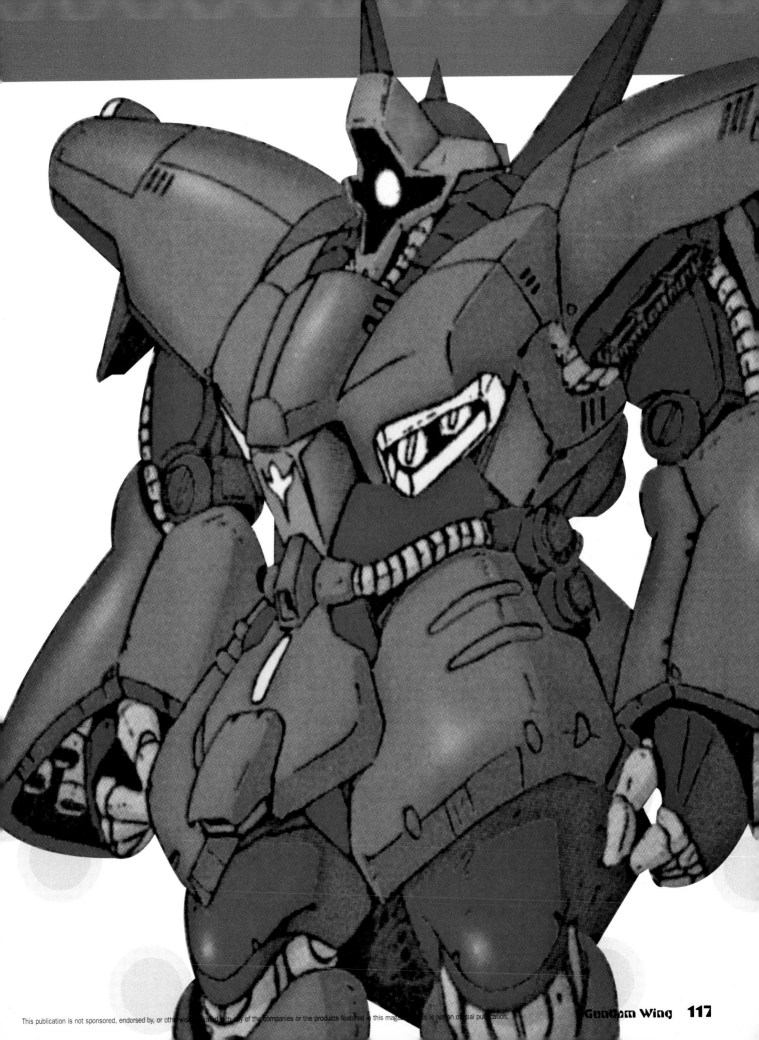

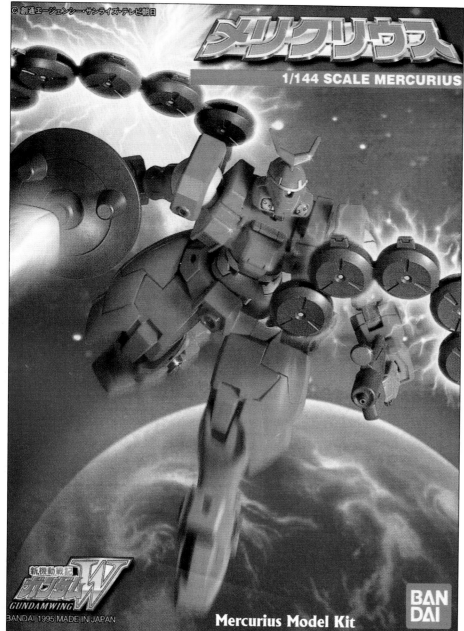

© 創通エージェンシー・サンライズ・テレビ朝日

メルクリウス

1/144 SCALE MERCURIUS

新機動戦記
GUNDAM WING
BANDAI 1995 MADE IN JAPAN

Mercurius Model Kit

BAN DAI

1/144 scale Rick Dom II
from the 0080 line

Kit-bash 1/144
Desert Zaku

Wave soft vinyl
1/144 Baund Doc

sandpaper. Don't worry if the sandpaper scratches the surface a bit; you can apply some wax or car polish and rub it in with a piece of cloth.

When you finish assembling, use the marker to ink in the panel lines. You can do as much or as little as you like. Some kits have excessive panel lines, and it won't be as nice if you ink in all of them.

Don't be too timid; mistakes can be easily erased by wiping them with tissue paper and rubbing alcohol (buy it in drugstores). In addition to the panel lines, the weapon can benefit from some highlighting.

Orange Belt

At this level, you'll want to buy a bottle of modeling glue. The best kind comes in a glass bottle and looks almost like water. It contains a lot of solvent and works by dissolving a bit of the surface and letting the plastic itself do the sticking part. A lot of hobby shops stock a gel-type glue that comes in a tube; it's not as suitable for Japanese kits. You probably want to have a couple of finished kits under your belt before you try gluing.

Wing Gundam

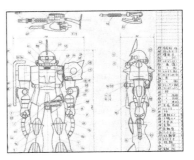

Zaku model design
from 1980

1/144 Gouf from the
08th MST line

Ready? Now as you assemble the parts, figure out which ones shouldn't be glued together (you may want to plan this ahead and mark the instructions with a pencil to remind yourself) and glue everything else. You especially want to glue the front and back halves of the torso and the left and right halves of the upper arms, forearms, thighs, calves and feet.

To glue two parts together, get everything ready (especially polycaps or other parts that need to go inside the parts you're gluing) and then apply a layer of glue all along the surfaces that are going to "kiss" when you put the parts together. You want to use enough glue so that when you press the parts together, a little bit of glue gets squeezed out all along the seam.

Now put the parts together and press hard. Don't touch the glue that was squeezed out. Put the parts down for at least 15 minutes. When the glue is completely dried, use sandpaper to remove the excess glue. If you do it right, the seam line will virtually disappear.

You'll find that some parts don't kiss perfectly. For those, the solution is not to apply more glue but to pull it apart again and inspect the parts for bits of plastic that may be getting in the way (they're called "flashes"). Clean them out with a knife or a small file. I have a habit of lightly sanding the kissing surface with a strip of 400-grade sandpaper, whether I see any flashes or not.

If the glue you applied earlier is already half dried, remove it completely before you re-apply the glue. Putting more glue on dried glue makes for a very ugly result. Gluing is a major skill; it'll take more than a few kits to master this art. Be patient and practice a lot.

Since the glue evaporates quickly, make sure you work in a well-ventilated room and take in some fresh air every 30 minutes or so. Your nose gets used to the smell quickly and you won't notice how much solvent you're sniffing. I'm serious – it'll dissolve your brain! Also, remember to keep your glue bottle tightly capped; otherwise, your glue will dissolve into thin air.

Red Belt

Now we're ready to paint. The easiest way is to use permanent markers. You can use any brand name, but Gundam Markers cover the widest range of colors. For painting, use the regular type of Gundam Markers, which have wide tips for covering large areas.

To get the best results, you need to use paints and brushes. Buy several brushes of different widths, and choose a brand of paint. Almost any brand designed for modeling will work fine. If you're just getting into painting, I'd recommend going with a water-soluble line of paints such as Testor ModelMaster or Gunze Sangyo Mr. Hobby Colors.

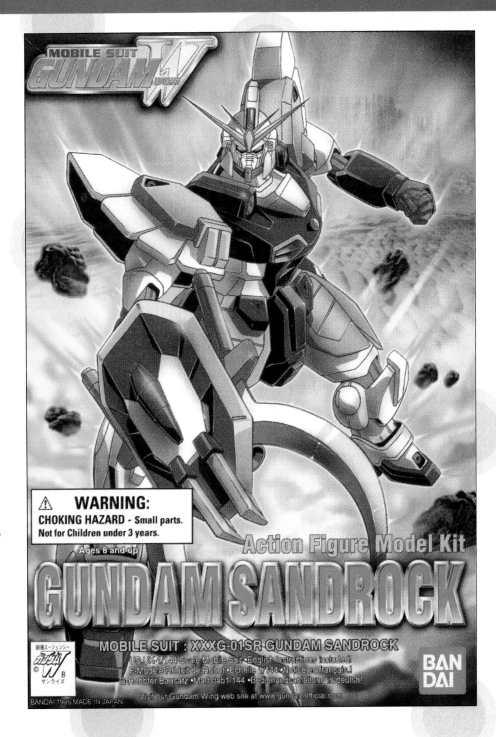

1/144 Gundam GP01 from the **High Grade Universal Century** line

Wind Zero Model Kit

WING GUNDAM 0

1/100 SCALE ウイングガンダム０

HG

BANDAI 1995 MADE IN JAPAN

BANDAI

third coat at a 45-degree angle to the last coat. By that time, all traces of brush strokes should be gone and you'll have a result no stickers could ever duplicate.

Brown Belt

Most people would be happy to be red belts, but if you want to build those "perfect" models like you see in *Hobby Japan* and *Dengeki Hobby*, take the next plunge. You need putty, files, sandpaper, primer, an air brush with a compressor and a lot of paints.

A brown belt would apply putty to all the gaps and surface defects; sandpaper all surfaces to a perfect finish; apply primer to everything and then airbrush everything, no matter how accurate the color of the original plastic is.

A brown belt also will airbrush in highlights, shadows and use dry brushing and washes where appropriate. Weathering is another necessary skill. And minor modifications are applied to almost every model – to the taste of the builder, of course.

Black Belt

Ah, so you want to be a black belt? Well, you won't learn it here. Black belts can't be taught; every black belt is a self-made man or woman. I can only tell you that a black belt creates and invents, rather than just building.

A black belt may build a different backpack or gun, a new head from scratch, change the proportions of the whole model or concoct a completely new paint scheme that reflects the personality of a particular character from a show or game. In short, a black belt doesn't reproduce something from the existing Gundam Universe; he/she creates something new that expands the Gundam Universe!

You should start with the easiest paint jobs, such as flat black for the area around the eyes, red or russet for jet exhausts, dark gray or steel for weapons and backpacks, and flat black inside the gun and cannon barrels. (Of course, you have to paint those before you assemble the guns).

When you're comfortable painting those areas, you can move on to larger areas. They tend to be more difficult because brush strokes tend to show up.

Remember to brush evenly in one direction only and wait for it to dry completely (overnight is best), and then brush evenly again at a right angle to the first coat. Wait for that to dry completely and, if necessary, paint a

Shopping Guide

Original (0079) – 1980

The original model series came out in 1980 and covered the TV series. By today's standards, this model series is considered low-grade. Most of the models are 1/144 scale, but there are quite a few 1/100-scale and 1/60-scale models as well. Gluing and painting are required, since most kits are molded in one color only.

The robot kits lack polycaps, and both proportions and posing are terrible compared with today's kits. Except for a few odd designs, almost none of the robots are recommended. But the nonrobot kits – ships, a tank, a fighter and several "Mobile Armors" – are very nice and are perfect for red belts looking for something different to add to their collections.

Unfortunately, after this original series, only a few nonrobot kits were sprinkled into the newer and better series. The Musai from this line is the best ship kit in the Gunpla world. Until recently, the small-scale models from this series were still selling well.

MS Variations (MSV) – 1983

MSV kits were launched in 1983. They're improved versions of 0079 kits, with more parts that produce better results. But they still require at least an orange belt to do it right. The mechas are mostly based on 0079 mechas, with a lot of extras and modifications done in a realistic military style. Today many kitbashers buy MSVs to get detailed parts to soup up the more basic newer kits. Personally, I love the Zaku Tank and Zaku Flipper from this line.

Zeta (Z) – 1985

Sometimes it feels like the Zeta TV series was created to sell models, which was true as far as Bandai was concerned. The series contains 36 kits, including a lot of interesting new designs. A major advance was polycaps (for improved articulation) on some models, but Z kits are still pretty tricky for anyone who is less than a red belt.

Double Zeta (ZZ) – 1986

Both the *ZZ* TV and model series are a direct continuation of *Z* Since only a few designs were introduced in ZZ, this is a relatively short model series. From 0079 to Z to ZZ, there was a gradual improvement in proportions and kit designs, along with a trend toward bigger, more fanciful designs with lots of odd bits. I love the EWAC-Zack (Eyezack) from this line, but other fancier designs from ZZ are also very nice.

Gundam Sentinel – 1987

Sentinel wasn't based on any animated show; it can be thought of as the MSV of ZZ, with even more odd bits, accessories and humongous guns. There are only five models, but they feature another technical advancement: system injection. All kits are equipped with polycaps.

Char's Counterattack – 1987

CCA features a lot of big mechas (22.5 m), so the models are bigger than before. CCA kits are the first fully snap-together ones, though they sometimes rely on screws to improve strength. They offer improved polycaps, designs and proportions, and they show a strong commitment to color molding, employing system injection to put several colors on the same runner.

This line has some nice models with good details and accessories that are good for orange belts and up. The 1/100-scale Nu-Gundam is one of the all-time favorites.

0080: War in the Pocket (0080) – 1989

The original video animation (OVA) story supposedly covered events in the same war as 0079, so the mechas should have been

1/144 EWAC-Zack (Eyezack) from the ZZ line

B-Club resin 1/144 Byarlant

1/144 GM from the 0080 War in the Pocket line

B-Club resin 1/144 Core Booster

1/1,200 Char's Musai from the Original (0079) line

the same. But the designers found some excuse to redesign all the mechas, so model fans are treated to a brand new line of nine models. The technical quality is very good – almost HG quality.

The parts are mostly molded in the right colors and require no glue. The Zeon MSs come with beautiful transparent pink monoeyes, and the two GMs come with transparent green visors. Several kits in this series are all-time favorites. Both GM-Command and Rick Dom II are great as either a first or second kit.

High Grade (HG) – 1990

With 10 years' worth of technological progress behind it, Bandai decided to introduce a "High Grade" label on a new line of models that revisits the old favorites from the first three TV series. The main feature of this line is true system injection. For the first time, several parts are molded in two or even three colors, making painting virtually unnecessary.

However, true system injection proved problematic from a quality-control standpoint, and it actually got in the way for brown-belt modelers who wanted to paint everything. So for later series, Bandai reverted to common system injection and stickers for color accuracy, which satisfied both lazy and serious modelers.

The original HG line contains only four kits (Gundam, Gundam Mk. II, Zeta Gundam and Gundam ZZ), but the "HG" label was later applied to every model line (F90, F91, SF91, V, W, EW, 08MST, HGUC) that has about the same technical features.

Still, if you line up all the HG models side by side, the quality varies. The Z and ZZ Gundams are transformable. Gundam Mk. II is an excellent kit for yellow belts. Gundam is not a great kit, but for yellow to red belts, it's a very good 1/144-scale rendition of the original hero.

Formula 91 (F91), F90 and Silhouette Formula 91 (SF91) – 1990

Suddenly, the robots are getting smaller instead of bigger – the typical mecha in the 0090s is only 15 m tall – so Bandai switched to 1/100 scale for its standard models. This is a nice line of lean-and-mean robots with big but realistic-looking guns. F90 and SF91 are sort of like the MSV of F91.

0083: Stardust Memory (0083) – 1991

A lot of fans in the U.S. were introduced to Gundam by this OVA series.

Unfortunately, this line is disappointing in both quality and selection. Many of the cool designs from the OVA were never made into plastic models. If you've seen this show on video and want to buy the robots, go for the Master Grade.

Victory Gundam (V) – 1993

Victory again features small (15 m) mechas, but unlike the F91/F90/SF91 lines, 1/144 is the standard scale. As a result, the models are very small (10 cm). Most employ a V-frame skeleton structure. Each model hangs different armor components on the same skeleton, so kitbashing possibilities are excellent.

The disadvantage is that all the models have the same size and proportions. Consequently, Bandai abandoned the V-frame, along with true system injection, for the later model lines. Some of the kits in this line are ugly, and a lot of the strange designs from the TV series weren't covered in the models. The overall picture is kind of disappointing. But V-Gundam and V2-

Gundam were released in a 1/100 HG line with several variations and transforming capability. Those are quite nice.

G Gundam (G) – 1994

The G Gundam mechas are slightly bigger than V mecha and the G Gundams also feature a lot of comical designs. These are nice kits, especially the 1/100 line, but only if you like the mecha designs.

Gundam Wing (W) – 1995

Anyway, back to the kits. This is an okay line of models. The 1/144-scale kits sometimes have problems with construction and posing, and they often require painting to look nice. The 1/100 HG kits are a lot better but, unfortunately, many bad-guy mechas aren't covered.

The Vayeate and Mercurius are covered in the 1/144, and the LM series covered the Leo and Taurus, but that's it for grunt mechas. This line is the only Gunpla being distributed domestically with English instructions and now English box art. However, if you can spring for an import, nab the recent reissue that comes with a 5-cm figure of your favorite Wing characters.

Master Grade (MG) – 1995

The MG series, like the HG line, revisited the old faithful: Gundams from the first few TV series and the main bad guys from 0079. This time around, Bandai went all out and recreated every detail in plastic moldings, in correct colors. These 1/100-scale (typically 18 to 20 cm) kits feature good posing, opening hatches, internal details, decals and stickers, and often other materials such as springs and meshes to recreate the finest details.

For many modelers, this is *the* line to get: The prices aren't exorbitant and the selection

isn't bad. And the kits are actually pretty easy to build. A yellow belt with some patience (each kit has 200 to 300 parts) can achieve an excellent result without any painting. In the hands of a more serious modeler who takes the time to clean up all the surface defects and paint the whole thing, these models can look impressive. The MG series pretty much set the standard for all sci-fi modeling in Japan.

Designing and sculpting each new MG kit requires a lot of time and money, so Bandai took its time releasing new MG models.

What's worse, a lot of those new models were simply color variants or MSVs with some extra gadgets thrown in. The selections were very conservative for almost four years, but fortunately, the release of the PG line in 1998 seems to have changed things a lot at Bandai. Now exciting new designs are coming out every few months, with variants to fill in the slower months. MG is going to be the staple line for Bandai for many years to come. Almost every kit in this line is recommended for yellow belts to black belts.

Gundam X (X) – 1996

The designs of this doomed TV series are similar to Wing designs, with a lot of big guns, fins and odd bits. The 1/144 line requires quite a bit of painting to look nice, but the 1/100 HG line is quite good. Bottom line: The designs are rather unusual and aren't for everybody.

08th MS Team (08MST) – 1996

This excellent OVA also spawned an excellent 1/144 model line. The mechas are faithful to the original 0079 designs, but the styling and details are brought up to a '90s standard, with an extra emphasis on military realism. The feel is very down to earth, much more like the infantry than an air/space force.

As the OVA release schedule dragged on (12 episodes in three years), the model releases also dragged out, taking

True System Injection from the High Grade line

three and a half years to release seven kits. But for many fans, the wait was worthwhile. The OVA may not have been a smash hit, but the 08MST models sold well enough to convince Bandai that another line of no-frills models of 08MST quality can be quite successful. The result was the HGUC line.

Just as some fans are turned off by the ornate designs of Wing and X, others are bored by the lack of flair in 08MST. Zaku F/J is a must-have because almost half the bad-guy mechas in the Gundam universe can be traced back to Zaku. The Gundam Ground Type vs. Zaku F/J double kit is also a good buy.

Endless Waltz (EW) – 1997

The sequel to the wildly popular Wing TV series was blessed with the redesigns of young mecha genius Hajime Katoki. The EW model line was likewise vastly improved over the Wing line, with better color molding, posing, proportions and details. The 1/144 models are just as detailed as the bigger 1/100 kits, so Bandai labeled both series "HG."

Many kits provide special "fighting-action" parts to recreate dramatic poses from the OVA. There was also a "special edition" of most of the kits, which has most of the parts molded in either colored transparent plastic or chromed in metallic paints. Watch out for the Tallgeese III kit. Unlike the rest of the series, Tallgeese III is just the old Tallgeese

I/II with extra parts thrown in for the new head and gun. Other than that, this is an excellent line.

Gundam Wing: G-Unit (GUNIT) – 1997

G-Unit was based on a comic side story in the Wing universe and was successful enough to spawn five model kits. The designs are rather wacky compared to other Gundam series. Technically, the models fall somewhere between Wing and EW. They're slightly below HG in toughness, so they're for orange- to red-belt modelers.

Perfect Grade (PG) – 1998

The success of the HG and MG lines proved to Bandai that 0079 fans are faithful and devoted customers. So, for the 20th anniversary celebration, Bandai looked beyond high grade and master grade and went straight for perfection. The first PG kit (the original Gundam, of course) costs Y12000 ($120!) and comes in a huge box. At 1/60 scale, it stands over 30 cm tall.

The amount of detail in this thing is almost insane; many seasoned modelers said they were exhausted by just the sheer size of the project. There are more than 600 parts, so assembly is a major undertaking, but everyone who did it said it's worth it.

The most amazing thing about the PG models – Gundam, Zaku (green), Char's Zaku (red) and Zeta Gundam – is that they can

strike almost any pose a human can. You can also get "custom sets" for Gundam and Zaku for extra weapons and transparent armors to show off the internal details. The next PG is Wing Gundam Zero Custom – it'll be a surefire hit on both sides of the ocean.

Turn-A Gundam (TA)

For this new TV series, American designer Syd Mead (Blade Runner) was invited to join the mecha design team. The result was some refreshing new ideas in Gundam designs. The funny mustache on the hero's head still has some oldtime fans (yours truly included) moaning and groaning, but everything else looks exotic and alien. Unfortunately, few designs were made into plastic kits. Turn-A Gundam (both 1/100 and 1/144 scale) is great.

High Grade Universal Century (HGUC)

These models mostly cover the earliest designs from 0079 and Z, which never got a good redesign in the previous HG and MG lines. For old-time fans, HGUC is a godsend. Highly recommended for white to black belts, Guncannon and Quebeley are special favorites. Guncannon and Gyan are great first kits.

First Grade (FG)

Back to the past for the future? The FG line brings back the 1/144-scale single-color plastic kits with beautiful PG-style

1/144-scale Guntank (left), Gundam (middle) and Guncannon models from the High Grade Universal Century line

1/144 Guncannon from the High Grade Universal Century line

proportions and details. The line also brings back the early '80s box-art style, price and technology (no polycap). Serious painting is required. Gluing is recommended. Highly recommended for red belts.

Superdeformed, BB Senshi and G-Generation

Superdeformed is one of those funky cultural gifts that Japan gave to the world. Any robot, no matter how steely and menacing, can be turned into a cute caricature with Pikachu proportions: huge head, simple body, small upper limbs, big feet, no legs. The guns and shields and the paraphernalia are big and exaggerated, and usually the gun is spring-loaded for shooting little missiles.

The BB Senshi (Baby Warrior) line of SD kits was designed to train young kids for bigger, more expensive models. The early BB Senshi kits were inexpensive and featured cute cartoonish box art; the instruction sheet had a one-page comic featuring a goofy adventure of the SD character. Though the model isn't very refined, it's easy to put together. Posing is limited – each one-piece arm can only swing up or down. The stickers provide various colors and often include a pair of big eyes for extra cuteness.

The latest SD releases are moving upscale. Some of these kits (including the G-Generation 0 line) are loaded with big-kit features like polycaps, color-accurate molding and crisp, sharp sculpting. Also gone are the

cutesy eyes, spring-loaded guns and comic-laden instructions. In their place are more funky accessories to play with. A few of these kits – like the RX-78-2, Zeta Gundam, GP-01Fb, GP-02A and GP-03D – are so big and mean that they more closely resemble MG kits.

Some would say they're not so cute anymore, but it's hard to argue with technical progress. All five are great as a first kit. The V2-Gundam is also great – it's smaller but truer to the original SD ideal.

A special subseries called the "Musha" (martial artist) is included, too. These are SD models with a lot of samurai-like ornamentation and sometimes even a horse to ride on. They're so popular with fans that there's even a comic series devoted to a Gundam/feudal-Japan universe.

High Complete Model (HCM)

Actually, HCMs are not models but toys that require some assembly. The HCM line also covers some non-Gundam robots like the Valkyrie from Macross.

Garage Kits (GK)

This is an entirely different category of modeling. Since plastic models don't cover every mecha design in the Gundam shows, a cottage industry has sprung up, run by black belts who cast their own sculptures for sale. Because the production runs are very short, the supply is very limited. The prices are very high, often reaching

Y10000 ($1,000) or more. There are two main types of GKs: resin and vinyl, with resin being by far the most common. Needless to say, GKs are for serious modelers only.

Surf This Way

With so many good Gunpla sites, it's almost unfair to list just a few. Besides these five, you can find many more on the links page at Newtype Asylum.

• Newtype Asylum (side7.gundam.com/newtype_asylum/): A site by Nightingale and myself. For modelers, we have reviews and resources such as color and instruction translations and a huge links page of other Gunpla sites.

• Church of the Machine (members. dencity.com/vovin/): This site by Joc Tejapaibul, a true black belt, has beautiful photos and a building diary.

• JAM (www.mars.dti.ne.jp/~jam/gm.html): This Japanese site by JAM, another black belt, has lots of pictures and a model-kit database.

• Mecha Domain (http://mechadomain. gundam.com/): Not a model site, but the best site for mecha references.

• Gundam.com (www.gundam.com): A general site with a model database and gallery. Gundam.com is the home of both Newtype Asylum and Mecha Domain.

C.T. (Core) Chin is a leading expert in Gundam modeling.

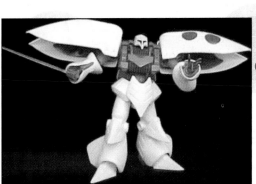

1/144 Quebley from the High Grade Universal Century line